# THE UNTRIED CASE

THE FOLLOWING PHOTOSTAT REPRODUCES
A LETTER WRITTEN BY JOSEPH B. ELY,
GOVERNOR OF MASSACHUSETTS, TO
HERBERT B. EHRMANN, ESQ.

THE GOVERNOR

THE COMMONWEALTH OF MASSACHUSETTS
EXECUTIVE DEPARTMENT
STATE HOUSE, BOSTON

September 27, 1933

Herbert B. Ehrmann, Esquire
14 Irving Street
Brookline, Massachusetts

Dear Herbert:

Before I read your new book "The Untried
Case" I had some doubt as to the guilt of Sacco
and Vanzetti. When I had finished, I had no
doubt of their innocence. The story is splen-
didly told and to one who had no background of
Sacco-Vanzetti history, it would also be most
interesting reading.

While in Chicago recently, I was somewhat
surprised to find a widespread feeling that the
decisions in the Sacco-Vanzetti cases were a
blot upon the judicial record of Massachusetts.
I do not feel that way about it because I have
always believed in the integrity of Judge Thayer
and of the justices of the higher court, although the result was quite likely a grave miscarriage of justice.

Sincerely yours,

Joseph B. Ely

# THE
# UNTRIED CASE

## The Sacco-Vanzetti Case
## and the Morelli Gang

by HERBERT B. EHRMANN

*Author of "The Criminal Courts of Cleveland";*
*Counsel, with William G. Thompson, for*
*Sacco and Vanzetti, 1926-1927*

*Foreword by*
JOSEPH N. WELCH

*Introduction by*
PROFESSOR EDMUND M. MORGAN

*Royall Professor of Law, Emeritus, Harvard University*
*Rand Professor of Law, Vanderbilt University*

•

THE VANGUARD PRESS, INC.     NEW YORK

*To*

WILLIAM G. THOMPSON

*who has vindicated anew the*
*finest tradition of the Bar*

# FOREWORD

THE COMMONWEALTH OF MASSACHUSETTS is, on the
whole, conservative. It is also reasonably law-abiding.
It has a good judicial system—not perfect but good.
The writer has moved in and out of its courtrooms for
forty years and has, for the most part, met upright
judges, courteous and fair opponents, and intelligent
juries.

In a rapidly changing world, it may be unsafe or
even dangerous to find oneself drawn to the conservative viewpoint. I have, however, always taken a quiet
satisfaction out of the phrase, "Massachusetts, there
she stands."

Massachusetts would not quickly be thought of as a
community that would produce three criminal trials
of truly legendary proportions. But Massachusetts has
succeeded in doing it.

The first trial, or, more properly, the first series of
trials, were the Salem witchcraft trials. The world will
never forget, or allow Massachusetts to forget, that we
solemnly executed persons of both sexes who had

been found guilty beyond a reasonable doubt of the crime of witchcraft.

The second Massachusetts criminal trial of legendary proportions was the trial of Lizzie Borden in Fall River for the crime of killing both her stepmother and her father with an ax. Many a child has recited the little verse:

> Lizzie Borden took an ax
> And hit her mother forty whacks;
> When she saw what she had done
> She hit her father forty-one.

It was never established that the facts stated in this little rhyme are accurate. Indeed, a jury found otherwise. If, however, there is such a thing as a "verdict of history," that verdict is that Lizzie was probably guilty. But, guilty or innocent, she has a place in our history and in our literature, including a moving and beautiful ballet by that great and compassionate choreographer, Agnes de Mille.

The third of the legendary criminal cases in Massachusetts is, of course, the Sacco-Vanzetti case. No other criminal case has ever attracted so much world-wide attention as this one. If it has a rival, which I think it does not, the rival would probably be the Dreyfus case. I am not forgetting that Pontius Pilate presided at a trial, never to be forgotten as long as Christianity endures. But that trial, followed by an execution, someway seems detached from the realm of criminal law and to belong solely to religion.

Why is it that Massachusetts will never be allowed
to forget its witches, its Lizzie Borden, and its Sacco
and Vanzetti? There are, I think, two principal reasons. One is that each situation involved the application, or possible application, of the death penalty. The
other is that each case involved a sharply divided public opinion with, let us say roughly, one half of the
community convinced of guilt and crying for revenge,
and the other half equally convinced of innocence and
terribly torn by the tragic consequences of the infliction
of the death penalty.

The number of people with a vivid personal memory
of the Sacco-Vanzetti case is now diminishing. Not
many have so vivid a memory as mine. I once lived in
Braintree. I then moved to Walpole and lived about
eight miles distant from the courthouse in which they
were tried and the jail in which they spent so many
bitter years. I knew William G. Thompson and held
him in the highest possible respect. His efforts on behalf of Sacco and Vanzetti were consistent with the
highest traditions of the Bar.

Herbert B. Ehrmann and I once worked in the same
office. He has been and is my friend. I also knew Judge
Webster Thayer. I have tried cases before him. I have
sat in his lobby and heard him discuss the Sacco and
Vanzetti case. It is clear that he believed Sacco and
Vanzetti to be guilty. It is also clear that this was not
merely an intellectual conclusion on his part, but a
passionate dedication to the proposition that the two of

them were to die. It was unfortunate that under Massachusetts law one man and only one man could grant Sacco and Vanzetti a new trial. That man was Judge Thayer. After the jury verdict, Judge Thayer's rulings on the various motions for a new trial were as fatal and as conclusive as was the throwing of the switch at their execution. But Judge Thayer was beyond persuasion. He was not to be moved by reason. He was, in this case, incapable of showing mercy. This is not to say he was wrong. It is only to describe him.

I have always thought that the great tragedy of the Sacco-Vanzetti case was that it happened to be assigned to Judge Thayer. I think almost any other judge would have granted a new trial. Assuming that Sacco and Vanzetti were as guilty as Judge Thayer believed them to be, a second jury would quite surely have found them guilty. If the evidence discovered after their conviction had been presented to a new jury with a unanimous verdict of not guilty, no one would have been dismayed. And in either event, with a second trial, no matter what the result, the conscience of Massachusetts would have been at rest.

The Braintree robbery and murders were committed by a gang of five men. It was what is called in police circles "a professional job." At the lowest that means that the adventure had to be planned, at least one car had to be stolen, roads had to be selected, and duties assigned to each of the five men involved.

Those who believe Sacco and Vanzetti were not

guilty are quick to point out that there is nothing to indicate that either of them had ever acquired any of the
special skills required in the successful planning of
this dangerous and complicated crime. No one has ever
suggested that either or both of them knew three cool,
skillful, and callous bandits who would join them in
this enterprise, which was to begin with the murder of
a paymaster and his guard. I would like to think that
Mr. Ehrmann and I are resourceful. But I would think
it quite beyond his power and mine to find three people
ready to join us in a payroll robbery and a double murder. There is nothing in the record or elsewhere to indicate that Sacco and Vanzetti knew their way around
in this very special field of crime, or how to find the
accomplices they needed.

The time came when a truly professional criminal
wrote a note saying that he was one of the five men who
staged the Braintree robbery and murders. The name of
this criminal was Celestino Madeiros. It is hard to see
how Madeiros could have thought this confession would
do him any good. Everyone who knew about it thought
it would do him immense harm, as in the end it did.
What Madeiros said did not have to be true just because it was dramatic. It was at first disbelieved by
counsel for Sacco and Vanzetti. But it *had to be* in-
vestigated.

This is the story of that investigation. It was made
by Mr. Ehrmann. He describes himself as an amateur,
which is not quite accurate, but he was far from a pro-

fessional investigator. His investigation had to be conducted privately, and he lacked the prestige that would have accompanied him had he been a member of the District Attorney's staff, or, let us say, a member of the State Police. Mr. Ehrmann, with the enthusiasm of youth and with complete devotion to Sacco and Vanzetti, whose counsel he was, did everything in his power to identify the five armed bandits who were of necessity implicated in the robbery and murders if the Madeiros confession was true.

This book was first published in 1933. Mr. Ehrmann then named five bandits who, he believed, "did the Braintree job." He was not sued for libel by any of the four then alive. This is not an impressive fact, since the men he identified had reputations so bad that no jury was apt to find they had suffered any injury by having someone say in print that they were both robbers and murderers. But Mr. Ehrmann is a man of honor. He would not accuse any man, no matter how despicable, of being a murderer without believing the accusation to be true. In the year 1927 Mr. Ehrmann thought he knew the names of the five men who murdered Alessandro Berardelli and Frederick A. Parmenter. He still thinks he knows, and the names Sacco and Vanzetti are not on Mr. Ehrmann's list.

JOSEPH N. WELCH

# PREFACE

IF SACCO and Vanzetti were innocent, who committed the murders for which they were executed?"

This question has been asked of me so frequently by persons informed about the Sacco-Vanzetti case that it is quite apparent the general public knows nothing of the evidence unearthed in 1926 and 1927 directly answering the inquiry. The history of the case, therefore, has seemed to me to require a volume dealing with this evidence, how it came to be gathered and how it was received by those charged with its consideration. As I was the person directly responsible for the investigation, I have undertaken to tell the story before memory and records grow indistinct. Because we of counsel for the defense were never permitted to submit the new evidence to a jury, I have entitled the book *The Untried Case.*

A few basic facts and dates may be of assistance to the reader in beginning the book. On December 24, 1919, there was an attempted hold-up of a pay-truck at Bridgewater, Massachusetts. On April 15,

1920, on Pearl Street, South Braintree, Massachusetts, a paymaster named Parmenter and his guard,
Berardelli, were shot to death in front of the Slater
and Morrill and the Rice and Hutchins Shoe factories.
These were the murders for which Sacco and Vanzetti were later executed. As the shots were fired, a
Buick automobile parked in front of the Slater and
Morrill factory started forward and as it passed the
scene of the crime, three bandits boarded it after toss-
ing the stolen money boxes into the tonneau. Before
picking up the bandits on the street, there were, according to the opening address of the District Attorney
at the trial, "two men in the car, the driver and a man
we cannot describe, in the back seat." The reader of
this book will judge as to the identity of this lone passenger. After the car was boarded by the killers, it
gathered speed and escaped. Two days later an abandoned Buick similar to the murder car was found in
the woods near Cochesett, about twenty miles away.

Sacco and Vanzetti were arrested on a street car,
May 5, 1920. Sacco was a shoe-worker, Vanzetti a
fish peddler, and neither had ever been accused of
crime prior to his arrest on this date. The police were
not specifically seeking them, and their arrest resulted
solely because they, with their friends Orciani and
Boda, had called for Boda's six-year-old Overland at
a West Bridgewater garage. This car was suspected in
connection with the South Braintree crime. However,
it was ruled out as evidence at the trial, no such

connection being established, and years later it was
shown that the car had not been operated all winter.
While being held on suspicion, Vanzetti was indicted
on June 11, 1920, for the Bridgewater attempt, and
convicted on July 1, 1920. Both Sacco and Vanzetti
were indicted for the South Braintree murders on
September 11, 1920, and convicted July 14, 1921.
There is no place in this prefatory note to consider the
evidence on which these convictions were obtained,
although some of it is necessarily referred to in the
story that follows. For a painstaking, disinterested
discussion, the latest book on the subject is recommended: *The Sacco-Vanzetti Case*, by Osmond K.
Fraenkel; [1] and for those who have the time to study
sources, *The Sacco-Vanzetti Case, Transcript of the
Record.*[2]

From July, 1921, to May, 1926, various unsuccessful efforts were made to obtain new trials for Sacco
and Vanzetti. Contrary to popular impression, Sacco
and Vanzetti were granted only the one trial which
terminated on July 14, 1921. All motions for a new
trial were denied by the same Judge, the Honorable
Webster Thayer, who presided over the case. Much
of the labor during this period fell to William G.
Thompson, one of the leaders of the Boston Bar. He
had not, however, represented Sacco and Vanzetti at
their trial. Counsel for the men on that occasion had

[1] Published by Alfred A. Knopf, 1931.
[2] Published by Henry Holt & Company, 1928.

been Fred H. Moore, Jeremiah J. McAnarney and Thomas F. McAnarney.

Meanwhile, on November 18, 1925, Celestino F. Madeiros, a professional criminal, confessed to his complicity in the South Braintree crime. Madeiros had been convicted of shooting fatally a cashier in an attempted bank robbery at Wrentham, Massachusetts, and was then awaiting the outcome of a bill of exceptions. He was granted a new trial, but was again convicted in May, 1926. Nothing was done about the confession until after this second trial of Madeiros; it was feared that if it were known he had admitted another murder, this might prejudice his chances with the new jury. Early in May, 1926, Mr. Thompson called on me to assist him in the defense of Sacco and Vanzetti, especially assigning to me the work of checking up the story of Madeiros. It is not an overstatement to say that both of us were amazed at what followed.

Mr. Thompson and I remained as counsel for Sacco and Vanzetti until shortly after August 3, 1927, when the appeal to Governor Alvan T. Fuller was denied. Thereupon we withdrew as counsel, feeling that perhaps fresh minds might accomplish more. The burden was then taken up by others led by Arthur D. Hill of the Boston Bar. Mr. Hill knew the cause was desperate, and fought for his clients courageously until the end. Our last appearance in the case was to plead before Governor Fuller, as private citizens, on the night of August 22, 1927, a few minutes before the men were electrocuted.

Perhaps a further personal word may not be entirely out of place. The Bar understands that the defense of clients does not imply agreement with their views, but many laymen make the mistake of assuming that lawyers for radicals must share their beliefs. Neither Mr. Thompson nor I belong even remotely to the school of thought represented by Sacco and Vanzetti, although we came to respect and admire them for their human qualities. As for myself, I am far more interested in the character of our citizenship than in any formulas for society. If the human material is right, we need not worry about the kind of system, because a people moulds society in its own image. For this reason I cannot agree with those who demand that the Sacco-Vanzetti case be forgotten. To forget is to invite repetition. The painful memory of past mistakes is the best teacher of humanity. Unfortunately, society finds it easier to erect statues to its martyrs than to recall the circumstances of the sacrifice. And yet the causes are invariably the same—minds that are closed by deep prejudice or transient passion. If, as in the case of Sacco and Vanzetti, the local hostility was inflamed by foolish words of their sympathizers or wicked deeds of their exploiters, this also is a fact to be recollected. Our vigilance to guard against injustice may be quickened by the memory that in 1927 the fine old Commonwealth of Massachusetts was diverted from its own high traditions by the howl of the pack to "show the Reds."

Until Governor Fuller's decision was released on August 3, 1927, Mr. Thompson and I refrained from any public comment. We believed that it was contrary to the ethics of our profession to try our case in the newspapers. The legal aspect of the case, however, has been closed by death, and our duty now is to the record of history. I have in mind, also, Vanzetti's last request of Mr. Thompson to "clear his name." The book is written in this spirit, but if it should be found to suffer from the unconscious faults of partisanship, then it may be remembered that the writer is firmly convinced that Sacco and Vanzetti not only did not, but that they could not, commit the crimes for which they were put to death.

HERBERT B. EHRMANN.

# PREFATORY NOTE

# TO SECOND EDITION

*The Untried Case* is a personal account of the evidence gathered in 1926 and 1927 implicating a Providence gang of professional criminals as the real perpetrators of the murders for which Sacco and Vanzetti were executed.

The original edition, published in 1933, has long ago been exhausted. Copies are no longer available to meet the rising tide of interest in the Sacco-Vanzetti case that has developed over the years.

The case against the Morelli gang of criminals appears to be far more complete and impressive than the evidence produced against the fish peddler and the shoemaker. Doubts concerning the guilt of Sacco and Vanzetti are therefore powerfully reinforced by the existence of proof of the identity of the real murderers. This makes the Sacco-Vanzetti proceedings unique among those celebrated cases that history has come to believe were miscarriages of justice.

Since 1933 the Sacco-Vanzetti case has been the subject of constant research and review. In all this time

not a single fact has been unearthed that, in any respect, weakens the massive case against the Morelli
gang.

Some efforts were made to induce Joseph Morelli,
the gang's chieftain, to admit his participation in the
crime. As was to be expected, these overtures were not
productive of self-incrimination. Nevertheless, abor-
tive as they were, they were not without significance.
For instance, a Providence reporter obtained a promise from Morelli's lawyer to let him know when and if
this criminal had something to say. When Morelli was
dying of cancer, the word finally came, and the reporter responded to the call. However, the family
would not admit him into the sick room until they could
contact the lawyer. This consumed several hours, and
when the reporter finally got permission, the dying
man had sunk into a coma.

Morris L. Ernst, Esquire, had extensive conversa-
tions with Joseph Morelli, who admitted complete familiarity with the details of the crime, some of which
had been unknown. Efforts to obtain a written confirmation, however, failed when Morelli put too high a
price on his story. A photostat of a letter from Morelli
to Mr. Ernst is included in the Appendix.

A new appendix is a letter written to me by Governor Joseph B. Ely, on State House stationery, September 27, 1933. Mr. Ely was one of the leading trial lawyers of Massachusetts and had been a District Attorney
himself. Therefore, the letter is impressive, especially

as it required moral courage for a Governor to state in writing that he was convinced of the innocence of Sacco and Vanzetti after his predecessor in that high office had permitted them to be electrocuted.

Further appended is a transcript of my remarks at the memorial to William G. Thompson before the Bar Association of the City of Boston. It seems to me to be appropriate that this estimate of a valiant champion of justice by his junior associate should be put in permanent form. The reader may also detect in my remarks that Mr. Thompson clearly perceived the malaise that afflicts the age in which we live.

The astonishing reaction of Justice Pierce to my memorial observations is added as a note to this appendix. Here is suggested another puzzling feature of the Sacco-Vanzetti tragedy—namely, a probable internal division among the Justices of the Massachusetts Supreme Judicial Court behind the decisions that presented the outward appearance of unanimity.

HERBERT B. EHRMANN

June 6, 1960

# INTRODUCTION

WHY a new edition of this volume that stirs again the ashes of the Sacco-Vanzetti case? Why persist in making obvious the perversion of justice that public hysteria and ignorant prejudice can produce even in a state with a background of culture and refinement blessed with unsurpassed institutions of learning dedicated to the pursuit of truth? Because in this instance the triumph of prejudice over reason affected the administration of justice throughout a process designed to furnish every safeguard against it, and demonstrated the futility of formal requirements to insure the enforcement of fundamental rights.

And certainly the current climate of opinion does not justify confidence that it may not happen again. This does not mean that the issue of guilt or innocence of an accused must or will be correctly resolved, but it does mean that an accused—every accused—shall be given a fair trial by an impartial tribunal. It also means that whatever procedure is provided for the review of the trial and for presentation of new matter

probative of innocence shall be open to the accused—
every accused—without discrimination against him
because he is the kind of man he happens to be or because he holds the views he happens to hold.

This book provides the conclusive evidence that
Sacco and Vanzetti were the victims of such discrimination by the trial judge in the post-conviction proceedings, and that the appellate tribunals found no
way to counteract it. It should be read against the
background of the evidence and rulings at the trial and
the judge's opinions in support of his denial of the
earlier applications for a new trial.

A careful reading of the trial record clearly reveals:
1. That the evidence of identification was weak and
unconvincing, though it was aided by testimony as to
a cap found at the scene of the killing that was about
the size of Sacco's cap and that had a tear in the lining,
caused, so the prosecution said, by the nail at the factory on which Sacco usually hung his cap while at
work. The one witness who claimed to have seen Sacco
near the bandit car and to have spoken to him before
the killing was Lola Andrews. She was squarely contradicted by the woman who accompanied her at the
time and was badly impeached by evidence of prior
contradictory statements and of bad reputation for
veracity. She was, however, rehabilitated by prosecutor Katzmann in his summing up, in which he said: "I
have been in this office, gentlemen, for now more than
eleven years. I cannot recall in that too-long service for

the Commonwealth that ever before I have laid eye or given ear to so convincing a witness as Lola Andrews." This was an outrageous breach of professional ethics and was prejudicial error as a matter of law, for he was giving character evidence without first being sworn as a witness, subject to cross-examination by the defendants; and had he been sworn, his evidence would have been inadmissible.

2. The subject of the radicalism of defendants was introduced by them. Counsel for the defense deemed it necessary to show that the numerous falsehoods the defendants had told after their arrest were caused by fear that they were being held in custody because of their radical views, as some of their friends had been in the then current series of arrests and prosecution directed by Attorney General Palmer. That the testimony was so ineffectively presented was due partly to the inexplicable obtuseness of the trial judge and his purported fantastic notion that the purpose of the defendants was to show that their efforts to collect and dispose of the subversive literature was to protect the United States government. The cross-examination of Sacco by Katzmann went to the very verge of the permissible, even assuming that it was to test the honesty of Sacco's professions of radicalism. Sacco had testified that he had come to this country in 1908 "because I was liked a free country." With this as a basis Katzmann conducted a cross-examination that covers some fourteen pages of the record and discloses many mis-

takes in Sacco's information concerning various opportunities open to people of his class for education and advancement, and particularly Sacco's pacifism and draft-dodging.

3. Almost every ruling on objections calling for the exercise of the discretion of the trial judge was against the defendants.

4. The case for the prosecution was handled with consummate skill; that for the defense with an ineptitude that is scarcely believable by those who knew and know the capacity of the McAnarney brothers as trial lawyers.

If the record is reread in connection with data presented in support of the motions for a new trial prior to that which is the subject of this book, the following disturbing facts appear without contradiction.

1. The testimony of the ballistic experts for the prosecution, which, if analyzed, would barely warrant a conclusion that the fatal bullet was fired from Sacco's pistol, is completely shattered by Proctor's affidavit. There can be little doubt that counsel for the defendants and the trial judge interpreted Proctor's testimony as expressing his opinion that the bullet had been fired from Sacco's pistol. In truth, his opinion was quite the contrary. He could find no evidence that indicated the bullet went through the barrel of Sacco's pistol. He had so informed counsel for the prosecution, and yet they presented him as a witness and put to him a question framed by arrangement in advance to enable him

to express a half truth, a half truth that had all the effect of a lie; and it requires an incredible naïveté to believe it was not intended to have that effect.

2. The tear in the lining of the cap was caused not by any nail upon which it might have been hung but by the police while searching for identifying marks. Even if this was not known to the prosecuting attorneys, the police could not have been unaware of it.

3. The prosecution knew of two witnesses who had ample opportunity for observation of the bandit whom Lola Andrews identified as Sacco, while he was about the bandit car before the killing, and knew they would testify that the bandit was not Sacco. The prosecution also knew of a witness who would testify that the bandit who was shooting from the car as it left after the killing passed within ten feet of him and fired a shot at him that went through the lining of his overcoat, and knew he would testify that that bandit was not Sacco. And yet they did not inform the defense of the existence of any one of these three witnesses.

With an attitude revealed by such conduct of the prosecution, as well as by Katzmann's illegal bolstering of Lola Andrews, can anyone be so witless as to believe his cross-examination of Sacco was for the legitimate purpose of testing the sincerity of his radicalism and not for the totally illegitimate purpose of directing against him the intense prejudice then prevalent against slackers and radicals?

4. The opinions of the trial judge in denying the

motions for a new trial are filled with prosy platitudes; each alleged ground asserted by the defense is treated as if it stood alone; at times the opinion reads like a brief for the prosecution. The combined opinions reveal a determination to uphold the convictions at all costs and contain many positively erroneous statements.

The disposition of the previous motions demonstrated the futility of efforts to show that Sacco and Vanzetti did not commit the murder and robbery. The Medeiros motion was an example of the Perry Mason technique—an effort to establish the identity of those who did commit these offenses. Let me repeat what I said when the original edition of this book appeared:

"This is an exciting tale well told. Beginning with a wholly worthless story from an utterly untrustworthy source, our investigator turns up clue after clue and fact after fact until he is transformed from an honest doubter into an enthusiastic convert. As he builds his case bit by bit against the Morelli gang; as bit by bit he tears away the supposed case against Sacco and Vanzetti; as he calls in his Sherlock Holmes to demonstrate the inherent verities in the confession of a convicted murderer and epileptic liar, the reader is swept along with him. Once let the prosecuting authorities of the Commonwealth of Massachusetts learn these facts, and soon the guilty Morellis will take the places of Sacco and Vanzetti. With all the resources of the state at their command they will assemble the witnesses and perfect the evidence and see that justice is done. Confidently our investigator calls upon them. With amazement he receives their response: 'We will answer, but not investigate, because we know or believe that the truth has been found.' "

Whether this response was justified, let the reader determine for himself.

E. M. MORGAN

Nashville, Tennessee
June 1, 1960

# CONTENTS

# CONTENTS

# THE UNTRIED CASE

# CHAPTER ONE

# A SLIP OF PAPER

DETECTIVE THOMAS F. DUGAN of the New York police was certainly not expecting anything to happen when he settled down to lunch on February 10, 1921. For comfort he had removed his belt, with holster and pistol, and hung them with his hat and overcoat on a hook nearby. It had been a humdrum morning, a drab wintry day. Boshen's German Restaurant on Broome Street, near Mulberry, stood almost in the shadow of the massive building which is the Police Headquarters of New York City—a spot, one would say, to be shunned by murderers. There was a sudden succession of sharp reports outside. Most of the guests assumed that they were hearing the backfiring of a motor. Detective Dugan, however, thought he heard something else and dashed around the corner to Mulberry Street. He scarcely had time to realize that he was without hat, overcoat—or pistol.

A man lay in the street mortally wounded. A woman with a seven-month-old baby was screaming that she had been shot. The fast gathering crowd was a chaotic mass of excited and panicky people. It was a strange scene to be enacted within pitching distance of the great police citadel just beyond. The perpetrator of this grim irony glided coolly into the crowd. Detective Dugan followed, but dared not show haste lest he warn the dangerous quarry. When the two came abreast, the man was walking leisurely along with a lighted cigarette in his mouth. Dugan grabbed the nonchalant murderer. Fortunately for the unarmed detective, the surprise capture prevented his prisoner from using again the murder weapon.

The pistol in question was a peculiar affair with a wooden handle and retained seven undischarged cartridges in the clip. More significant, however: it was a foreign automatic, 7.65 millimeter calibre, through which were fired bullets of American .32 calibre. Detective Dugan had captured Antonio Mancini, of Providence, Rhode Island, listed as a "spaghetti importer" but known to his associates and the police of that city as a quiet gunman with an iron nerve.

It was most unfortunate for Sacco and Vanzetti, then facing trial in Massachusetts for a double murder at South Braintree, committed with the same characteristic audacity and indifference, that their expert witnesses did not have before them the curious weapon retrieved that morning in Mulberry Street. It is at least possible that the court and the jury in their case would have listened with much attention to

evidence that five of the bullets taken from the bodies
of Parmenter and Berardelli, killed at South Braintree, were of thirty-two calibre fired through a foreign
7.65 millimeters, and that shells found on the scene
bore an ejector-claw mark utterly unknown to any
American pistol.

At the trial, and for five years thereafter, such evidence seemed without significance, since both State
and defense were discussing an unknown weapon in
the hands of an unknown killer. Had Mancini been
suspected at the time, the jury might have preferred
to believe that the man who calmly murdered on a
busy street in New York was more likely to have committed the public killings in South Braintree than the
fish pedler and shoemaker whom they convicted. This
preference might have grown to a belief, had they
known further that Antonio Mancini lived in Providence, Rhode Island, where he was rated a "big job"
member of the notorious "Joe Morelli gang," professionals in nearly all branches of criminality. The
belief might have become conviction had it been
known that another gunman would confess to his part
in the South Braintree murders and implicate the
"Morelli mob" as the guilty gang.

But there was no one in 1921, or for years thereafter, to whisper of any possible connection between
the murder of Alberto Alterio on Mulberry Street,
New York, and the shooting of Alessandro Berardelli
on Pearl Street, South Braintree, on April 15, 1920.

On November 18, 1925, however, Celestino F. Madeiros, a young bank robber and confessed murderer, confined in the Dedham jail where Sacco was imprisoned, succeeded in smuggling into Sacco's cell a slip of paper which began an investigation and opened wide an entirely new phase of the Sacco and Vanzetti case. The circumstances surrounding this confession will be examined later. The paper bore the following words written in the handwriting of Madeiros: "I hearby confess to being in the South Braintree shoe company crime and Sacco and Vanzetti was not in said crime."

The paper was delivered to William G. Thompson, attorney for Sacco and Vanzetti since their conviction, who promptly interviewed Madeiros, taking notes and sending copy to the District Attorney. Nothing further was done at the time, however, because Madeiros was awaiting the outcome of his appeal from a conviction for murder and it was thought that public knowledge of his confession to still another murder might prejudice his chances should a new trial be granted. The exceptions of Madeiros were sustained by the Supreme Judicial Court and Madeiros was granted a second trial in May, 1926, and convicted again. Meanwhile Mr. Thompson's plea for a new trial in behalf of Sacco and Vanzetti before the same appellate court was rejected, and thereupon the Madeiros confession became of great and immediate importance.

At this juncture Mr. Thompson asked me to assist
him in the investigation. The burden of carrying on
alone had become almost intolerable after three years
of unsparing devotion to the task of obtaining a second trial for his clients. As my practice was largely
of a business nature with practically no criminal cases,
I was at a loss to know why I had been recommended
to him unless it was because of my study of the
Criminal Courts of Cleveland in 1920. Nevertheless,
it was a call which I could not refuse and my acceptance began one of the most valued associations of my
life.

It thus happened that on May 22, 1926, I left the
relative quiet of an office practice and found myself
on my way to Providence, bound for the Bluebird
Inn, a disreputable roadhouse in the lonely hamlet
of Seekonk. It was to be my first port of call on a long
voyage. On that spring afternoon, however, I was
wholly skeptical of the Madeiros story and confidently
expected that the quest would end in a few days. If
Madeiros were not telling the truth, the check-up
would speedily tell. In his interview with Mr. Thompson, Madeiros had implicated an unidentified gang as
his associates who "had been engaged in robbing
freight cars in Providence." I expected to find that
there was no such gang; or, if it existed, that the
members were not Italians; or, if Italians, that they
were not available for committing the crime on April
15, 1920. The chances were slim for a manufactured

story to click on coincidences. Even so, however, I was not prepared to believe Madeiros merely because his story might stand the first test. There might be other explanations. My disbelief in Madeiros was not based on any suspicion of the circumstances surrounding his confession. His was not a "death-house" confession in any sense of the word, and all agreed at the time that the statement was injurious to Madeiros, not helpful. My distrust was simply the normal skepticism of anything which looks "too good to be true." Lacking the knowledge of the history of the confession which we acquired later, I provisionally explained it to myself as proceeding from a desire for notoriety.

Nor did my hesitation to believe Madeiros spring from any belief in the guilt of Sacco and Vanzetti. On that May afternoon in 1926 I did not have the conviction which later possessed me that Nicola Sacco and Bartolomeo Vanzetti could not possibly have committed the murders in South Braintree. That was to grow with intimate knowledge of the men, a more seasoned understanding of the court record, and the development of new evidence. I did feel, however, that the talk of a "fair trial," however sincere, was self-deception if it meant anything beyond an observance of the forms of criminal procedure. It seemed to me that these two foreign radical draft-dodgers had been tried in an atmosphere where patriotism and justice became synonymous, where fear had replaced confidence, and where rumor raced through the corridors even to the Judge's chamber, rivaling the sworn testimony of the witness stand. In order to understand the investigation, as well as my doubts as to the guilt of the convicted men, it will be necessary to fix in mind a few simple facts concerning the double murder at South Braintree.

At the trial it appeared that the crime took place just before 3 P.M. on the afternoon of April 15, 1920. About 9.25 A.M. of that day the payroll money, $15,776, arrived from Boston in a box and was taken to an office across from the station to be assorted into pay envelopes for later delivery to the factory. As the expressman delivered the box of money, he observed what proved later to be the murder car, a newly varnished Buick (stolen a few months before) standing directly in front of the building. A man, later identified as the driver, stood in the doorway and another man sat in the car. The money was arranged in the office for the Slater and Morrill payroll, first into envelopes, the envelopes into wooden boxes, and the boxes into two steel cases, 2 feet long, 1 foot high, and 8 inches wide. At five minutes of 3 P.M., Parmenter, assistant paymaster of Slater and Morrill, and Berardelli, his guard, called for the boxes to carry them to the factory.

These two men proceeded east on Pearl Street, passing the Rice and Hutchins shoe factory, which was on the same side of the street as the Slater and Morrill factory and two hundred feet nearer. At this point

# ESCAPE ROUTE OF BANDITS

A-E   Section was established as the route by various witnesses.

E-F   Section is conjectural, but a government witness claimed to have seen the car at F, Matfield crossing, going around the loop.

F-G   Section is conjectural but is the logical route to Providence from Matfield based on Madeiros' story of the flight. It should be noted that, except for the vicinity of Bridgewater, these roads pass through no settled communities whatsoever.

B   is the hairpin turn by which the bandits threw off their pursuers who continued south to Holbrook.

C   is the Oak Street woods where Madeiros claimed the cars were exchanged.

D   is the fork at Oak and Orchard Streets where the car stopped before the home of Mrs. Hewins.

E   is the vicinity of the swing to the east. To have continued south would have brought the bandits into the city of Taunton; southwest into the Attleboros; west to the much traveled main artery to Providence.

I   is Cochesett where Vanzetti's friends Coacci and Boda lived and had kept their six-year-old Overland. Less than two miles away is the Manley Woods where the abandoned Buick was found, claimed to be the murder car.

J   is the hamlet of Seekonk where Madeiros later officiated as bouncer of the Bluebird Inn and marks the region used as a base for Madeiros and his associates in their attempt to rob the Wrentham National Bank in 1924.

The entire route discloses much forethought as it avoids communities and the traveled roads almost entirely. The "Old Post Road" is wild and lonely through most of its length and seems straight as an arrow to the motorist.

The easy access from New Bedford to the Manley Woods near Cochesett is also indicated.

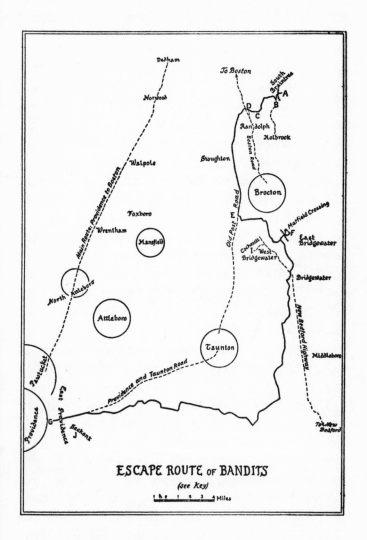

Dedham

To Boston

South Braintree

Norwood

D
C
B
A

Randolph
Holbrook

Walpole

Stoughton

Boston Road

Brocton

Foxboro

Wrentham

Mansfield

Old Post Road

E

Matfield Crossing

F
East
Bridgewater

Cochesett
I West
Bridgewater

North Attleboro

Bridgewater

Attleboro

New Bedford Highway

Taunton

Middleboro

Pawtucket

East Providence

Providence and Taunton Road

Providence

G

Seekonk

J

To New
Bedford

Main Route, Providence to Boston

# ESCAPE ROUTE OF BANDITS
### (see Key)

Miles

they were shot down by two bandits who had apparently been awaiting their arrival, described in the opening address of the prosecution as "two short men, perhaps five feet six or seven, rather stocky . . . between 140 and 160 . . . of apparent Italian lineage." While this was going on, the murder car was parked just beyond, below the Slater and Morrill factory, facing west, viz., toward the shooting. As Berardelli fell, the car crawled forward toward the scene. "There were two men in the car, the driver and a man we cannot describe in the back seat." As the car moved along, the two killers piled the boxes in, and with a third bandit boarded the moving car. The shooting had attracted swift attention, and people filled the windows in the factories and crowded the street where they were intimidated by shots from the car. The rear glass had been removed from the back curtain through which a weapon projected to cover pursuit. The occupants also scattered rubber-headed tacks in their trail to puncture tires of pursuing motor vehicles.

The car gathered headway, reached the main corner of the town, turned a right angle, sped south toward Holbrook about a quarter-mile, then made a hairpin turn, raced back into South Braintree, turned west and escaped through Randolph and south along an old but deserted and neglected highway. This daring ruse of doubling back into the town successfully threw off pursuit, as the police continued south into Holbrook. Two days later a car, claimed to be the murder car, was found abandoned in the woods not far from the route of escape, but about eighteen miles from the scene of the crime. On the night of May 5, Sacco and Vanzetti were arrested on an interurban street car by a single policeman.

Now, passing over the mass of conflicting evidence, which I had not yet digested, as to identification, expert opinion, and why Sacco and Vanzetti told falsehoods and were armed, I could not accept them as likely perpetrators of the job just described. The thorough planning and scouting, perfectly timed execution, and business-like killing in typical gangster fashion convinced me that professionals had done the job.[1] Sacco was an industrious, trusted shoeworker with a family, and Vanzetti was a visionary fish peddler "preaching to scorning men." Neither had ever been accused of any crime before their arrest on May 5. Vanzetti, it is true, had been tried and convicted, shortly after his arrest, of an attempted highway robbery at Bridgewater, but this verdict also rested on questionable identification.[2] It seemed incredible that

[1] The same opinion was held by Captain Proctor, head of the State police, and by the older men in the Department of Justice.
[2] The discovery in 1927 of reports made by Pinkerton detectives in December, 1919, and January, 1920, following the Bridgewater crime, shatter the identification testimony given at the trial. "There can be little doubt that if they [Pinkerton reports] had been available to the defence at the trial in Plymouth the identification testimony against Vanzetti would have been discredited, so great are the discrepancies between the statements made to these detectives and the

two such men could have had the will or the criminal
experience to perpetrate the Braintree crime. Moreover, it was unlikely that the April 15th murderers
should permit themselves to be arrested by one policeman. It is true that the officer testified that the defendants made movements as if to draw weapons.
Even if this testimony were not the usual police em-
bellishment of an arrest story—Sacco and Vanzetti
vigorously denied the claim—it would seem that the
bandits of South Braintree would have shot it out
instantaneously. It also seemed improbable that the
criminals, admittedly either automobile thieves themselves or closely associated with such, should be compelled to seek the use of a friend's broken down
"junk" and, failing this, should ride around on street
cars. Payroll robbers did not do that sort of thing—
especially successful ones.

My doubts were deepened by the complete failure
to connect Sacco or Vanzetti with any of the stolen
money. As Sacco had accumulated fifteen hundred
dollars in a savings account from his earnings, there
was no desperate need in his case. Vanzetti had continued his simple life, requiring little for his own
needs and collecting small sums for the assistance of
imprisoned radical friends.[3] A further indication that

testimony given at the trial." *The Sacco-Vanzetti Case*, by Osmond K.
Fraenkel, 1931, p. 159.

[3] The Commonwealth at first suspected that the defendants' friend,
Coacci, deported on April 16, 1920, had shipped the loot in his trunk,
but when it was intercepted, nothing suspicious was found. It was

something was wrong with the State's theory lay in
the fact that in five years the police had made no
apparent effort to apprehend a minimum of three
other bandits admittedly concerned in the crime. The
associates of Sacco and Vanzetti were well known, but
their alleged complicity never got beyond the corridor
of the courthouse.[4]

Skepticism as to Madeiros and doubts as to Sacco
and Vanzetti largely occupied my thoughts as I swung
off the main road toward Seekonk and East Providence in search of the Bluebird Inn. It was at this
roadhouse that Madeiros had worked prior to the
murder and attempted bank robbery which landed
him in the Dedham jail. Here he had been a chauffeur
by day, a bouncer by night, a bad man hired to keep
order among bad men. I hoped to obtain a few clues
from his employers after contact and confidence were
established. For if Madeiros were telling the truth,
it was likely that he had told the story before.

My inquiries as to the location of the Bluebird Inn

then whispered that Vanzetti had delivered the money to radicals in
New York. This rumor persisted until on the day preceding the
execution, August 22, 1927, the Department of Justice issued a statement that it had made an investigation into this subject at the request
of the District Attorney and had found no evidence of the existence
of such funds.

[4] Of the three friends suspected, Orciani was arrested and released
because of his alibi; Boda, who owned the ancient Overland car, bore
no resemblance to any described bandit; and Coacci, the deported
radical, who had resided with Boda, failed to fulfill police expecta-
tions when his trunk was seized and searched.

kindled suspicious gleams in the eyes of accosted citizens, but finally I came to the immediate vicinity. One last query for the place brought the news that it had been closed by the police, but possibly I would find what I wanted anyway.

To the passing eye, the Bluebird Inn looked like the usual New England farmhouse in the less desirable neighborhoods. It was frame and rambly, with a few chickens scratching about the place. As the kitchen door was open, I went up and knocked. I was a little surprised when the response came in the form of an old woman, brown as the earth, slender as a débutante, with a flaming cloth around her head and a bowl containing a half-picked fowl under her arm. She was a Brava, a member of that strange race of island Portuguese who for some reason appear in this section of Massachusetts. At the time I did not know that Barney Monterio, proprietor of the Bluebird Inn, was a Brava. When I asked for Mr. Monterio, the little brown woman invited me into the kitchen and vanished through a door. Within a few moments her exact opposite appeared, a strong, handsome young woman with the white skin, light eyes and blond hair of a Wagnerian heroine.

"Mr. Monterio is not at home," she said. "I am Mrs. Monterio."

My explanation of the purpose of my visit aroused no enthusiasm. She did not wince at the names of Sacco and Vanzetti as did many others in more con-

ventional walks of life, but her expression remained
serious and impassive. Of course, a stranger suddenly appearing and asking for information at a
roadhouse should not expect to be greeted with con-
fidences on the first visit. I said as much, but got
no response. Trying a new approach, I told her that
I had just left Madeiros. This started a series of
questions as to how he looked, where I saw him,
whether he was thin or ill, was there a chance of
his escaping the chair, did I think it right to execute
a man who was not quite sane, and so on, until, without any spoken invitation to come in, we conversed
ourselves out of the kitchen, across the dance floor,
past the piano to a dining alcove beyond. Her ani-
mated interest in Madeiros was a minor revelation
to me. The slouching animal I had seen in the courtroom cage the day before, gazing sullenly at the
judge and jury, presently became transformed into
a human being through the concerned eyes of his
friend, the mistress of the Inn.

# CHAPTER TWO

# THE BOUNCER OF THE

# BLUEBIRD INN

MAD, BAD, and dangerous to know!" These words, spoken lightly of Lord Byron, aptly describe the obscure Madeiros whose statement had sent me to the Bluebird Inn. From what Mrs. Monterio told me, and from many other sources, it is now possible to retrace the story of this criminal from his birth to the date when a few words scribbled on a slip of paper swung his fate into the same rhythm as that of Sacco and Vanzetti. The story of the investigation would be incomplete without a view of the man who started it and the circumstances surrounding his confession.

Celestino F. Madeiros was born at Villa Franca, San Miquel of the Azores Islands, March 9, 1902, one of nine children. His parents were farm hands in their native country but emigrated to America when Celestino was two or three years old, settling in New Bedford, Massachusetts. Here the boy went to school from the age of five or six years until he was fifteen, but not continuously. From his earliest school days Celestino suffered from very bad eyesight, going

30

"blind" for extended periods, and doing poorly in those subjects requiring the use of his eyes. Because of this defect it was at first thought that the lad was subnormal in intelligence, but as he matured this apparent subnormality gradually disappeared. At the time of his trial in May, 1926, he rated at least average intelligence, if not higher. A few weeks later he faced a cross-examination by Mr. Thompson and, although he had set himself an impossible task, as will be seen, he gave an exhibition of mental fencing that would have reflected credit on a trained intelligence.

A graver defect than poor vision, however, afflicted this young man. Like Oswald in Ibsen's *Ghosts*, he was worm-eaten from birth. His father had been subject to "fits." A paternal aunt and uncle had died in Portugal, simple minded. His mother's sister had died insane. His mother, a pathetic figure on the witness stand, had testified that she also was subject to "fits" which had lately increased in frequency "because of the boy." A short time thereafter she was suddenly heard to emit the characteristic groan of the epileptic, and was carried unconscious from the courtroom, twitching in every muscle and foaming at the mouth. Celestino himself suffered from *le petit mal*, a form of epilepsy marked by momentary losses of consciousness. A juvenile delinquent at the age of fourteen, with a record of twelve previous arrests and convictions, his reputation for acts of violence was even greater among his associates than with the police. Another characteristic was a poor memory for dates and details which, as will be seen, was later seized upon as proof that Madeiros was lying.[1] By that time, however, we no longer needed to rely upon Madeiros, so strong was the extrinsic proof of his story.

The alienists agreed that Madeiros was sane in a legal sense, but called him a "psychopathic personality," whatever that may mean. One of his peculiarities was a taste for firearms. As if to compensate himself for the wrongs nature and society had done to him, Madeiros accumulated bigger and better pistols. When, in November, 1924, he shocked the peaceful townsfolk of Wrentham by walking into the little National Bank and shooting the aged cashier, he carried and fired a revolver of forty-five calibre. This same weapon had been used by him in a lighter mood to shoot flies off the ceiling at the home of his friend, James F. Weeks. At the Bluebird Inn he had constantly practiced with a thirty-eight calibre revolver, on one occasion outraging Mrs. Monterio by killing her cat and its three kittens. One evening he had stood before the Inn, pistol in hand, and defied a gang of twelve Italians who had come to take away a girl named Tessie. The identity of the gang and the significant remark of Madeiros will be considered later. After leaving the employ of the Inn, Madeiros re-

[1] Periods of dangerous violence and defective memory are frequently associated with *le petit mal*, according to the Encyclopedia Britannica, eleventh edition, vol. IX, p. 692.

turned one night and engaged in a pistol duel with
Barney Monterio. Mrs. Monterio did not tell me the
cause, but as Madeiros later stated that he had un-
successfully besought her to elope with him, one
suspects the old, old story. On two other occasions Madeiros was "mixed up" in shootings—this in addition to rum-running, hi-jacking, and robbery. While
in the Dedham jail he made a violent effort to escape,
which nearly cost the life of a guard.

Faithfulness to the code of the gangster was an
outstanding quality of Madeiros. The criminologist
may well ponder the misdirected but outstanding
courage and loyalty of this murderer. The latter quality proved a source of some embarrassment to Mr.
Thompson and myself in the beginning of the investigation and made Madeiros an unwilling witness. He
wanted to tell enough to save Sacco because he "felt
sorry for Mrs. Sacco and the kids," [2] but he tried to
avoid directly naming or identifying his associates.
"If I cannot save Sacco and Vanzetti by my own confession, why should I bring four or five others into
it?" He was willing to give us enough to make our
own investigation and apparently had no objection
to others telling what they knew. Neither in his first
statement to Mr. Thompson nor in his cross-exami-

[2] Mrs. Sacco was a young woman of considerable charm and refinement. In the happier days she had acted with her husband in amateur
benefit performances. The beauty of their two children, Dante, and
Inez (born after Nicola's arrest) was a continuous subject of comment
by all who saw them.

nation at a later date, did he call the gang by name.
He identified it "off the record," however, by name
and more formally by complete and accurate description. When it came to the names and addresses of his
individual associates, Madeiros at first made misleading statements, but under cross-examination was compelled to admit that he had attempted to screen their
identity from Mr. Thompson. This attitude of Madeiros made it easy to discredit his story—provided
one ignored all the other facts connected with it.

The various attempts of Madeiros to give information to Sacco indicate clearly his peculiar attitude.
At first he merely suggested to Sacco to send to a boy
named "Thomas" in Randolph. This was during Madeiros' first trial, long before the actual confession.
At this time he occupied the cell next to that of Sacco.
Subsequently, he sent to Sacco a plan of Oak Street
in Randolph, on a yellow sheet of paper, with the
residence of Thomas marked with a cross. This he did
in the hope that the boy, if visited, would say that
he had seen the murder car pass his house on Oak
Street after the crime and that he had recognized
people in the car.[3] Thus Sacco's friends would be led

[3] Later I interviewed young Thomas who maintained that he did not
recollect seeing the car, but that his mother had seen it. His mother,
however, was now dead. Thomas had just secured a good position
with a large corporation and I sensed his fear that further publicity
would hurt his future. James F. Weeks, associate of Madeiros in the
Wrentham job, had been arrested in Thomas' home and the resulting
notoriety had greatly humiliated his family.

to start their own investigation and relieve Madeiros
of an unprofessional confession. Sacco, however, paid
no attention to Madeiros and destroyed the plan. He
knew that the State, in cooperation with the Federal
Government, had placed a spy in the cell next to his
and thereafter he distrusted all efforts by inmates to
communicate with him.[4] On subsequent occasions, in
the bathroom and while exercising below Sacco's cell,
Maderios would say, "Nick, I know who did the South
Braintree job." Sacco, still unbelieving, ignored him,
except that on one occasion he reported the matter to
Mr. Crocker, the night officer, who recalled the incident months later. As nothing resulted from these efforts, Madeiros then decided that the time had come
for him to confess. On November 16, 1926, he addressed an envelope to the *Boston American* and en-
closed the following statement:

"Dear Editor:
I hearby confess to being in the shoe company crime at
South Braintree on April 15, 1920, and that Sacco and Van-
zetti was not there.
                              CELESTINO F. MADEIROS."

[4] The placing of the spy, Carbone, next to Sacco's cell and the activities of the agents of the Department of Justice generally constitute
another unusual phase of this case. One detective swore that the
prosecutor proposed planting him as a boarder in Mrs. Sacco's home to
obtain confidential information from her by taking advantage of her
distressed mental state. The District Attorney denied discussing such
a plan, but admitted the interview.

This letter reached Deputy Sheriff Curtis that same afternoon, but got no farther.[5] When Madeiros found that his communication to the *Boston American* had not left the jail, he wrote out the slip of paper mentioned in the preceding chapter and sent it to Sacco by a runner named Miller.

"I have never been intimate or chummy with Sacco since I came here," said Miller subsequently. "He avoids the other prisoners and keeps by himself, and is not chummy with anybody so far as I know.

"On November 18, 1925, while acting as trusty or runner, I got a 'rap', as we call it, from the cell of Madeiros. I went there and he handed me a slip of paper and asked me to give it to Sacco. I read it. I cannot from memory give the exact wording of the paper, but it was a confession that he was in the South Braintree job and that Sacco and Vanzetti had nothing to do with it. It was a small, oblong piece of paper. At that time and at present Madeiros was confined in a cell on the ground floor or lower part of the jail. On coming up the steps from this part of the jail with the paper given me by Madeiros in my possession, I heard a rap from the other side of the jail on tier No. 2 on the back, and went there before going to the cell of Sacco. The man in that cell, whose name I don't

---

[5] No legal or ethical justification has ever been offered for withholding from defense counsel such an important document, or information about it. Yet this same Mr. Curtis, on a hot summer's day, trudged several blocks to Dedham Centre and back again to procure ice-cream for Sacco and Vanzetti and "stood the treat" himself.

remember, handed me a magazine and asked me to give it to Sacco. I put the slip of paper given me by Madeiros between the leaves of the magazine handed me by the other man, and handed the magazine to Sacco and told him there was a note inside. This was in the afternoon.

"A few minutes later I went to Sacco's cell and he was standing leaning against the wall trembling, with the paper in his hands sent to him by Madeiros, and tears in his eyes. He asked me, 'What is this?' I said, 'Can't you read English?' He said he would telephone his friend and get him to take the paper to Mr. Thompson."

And so, after efforts continuing over several months, Madeiros finally succeeded in getting his vital message to persons who would investigate his story. Mr. Thompson immediately obtained permission to interview Madeiros and did so, in the open rotunda of the Dedham jail. For the moral effect, Sacco also sat at the table where he exhorted Madeiros to tell the truth "for Jesus' sake." This is the story he told to Mr. Thompson on November 19, 1925:

"On April 15, 1920, I was picked up at about 4 A.M. at my boarding house,[6] 181 North Main Street, Providence, by four Italians[7] who came in a Hudson

[6] Later he said the meeting place was across the street from his boarding house, at a barroom—"figure that's the same thing."

[7] Later Madeiros said this was an error, as one of the four, the driver of the car, was a Pole or Finn.

five passenger open touring car. The landlord of my boarding house was a Jew whose name I do not remember. One of my sisters lived at the same place. She was then a widow and her name was Mary Bover. She has since been married, and now lives at 735 Bellville Avenue, New Bedford. There was also living there at the same time a man named Arthur Tatro, who afterward committed suicide in the New Bedford House of Correction. He was Captain and I was a Lieutenant in the American Rescue League at that time. Two or three privates in the League also lived there, whose names I do not remember.

"We went from Providence to Randolph, where we changed to a Buick car brought there by another Italian. We left the Hudson car in the woods and took it again after we did the job, leaving the Buick in the woods in charge of one man, who drove it off to another part of the woods, as I understood.

"After we did the job at South Braintree and changed back into the Hudson car at Randolph, we drove very fast through Randolph, and were seen by a boy named Thomas and his sister. His father lives on a street that I think is called Oak Street, and is in the window metal business or something of that kind. I became acquainted with him four years later when I went to live in Randolph with Weeks on the same street. Thomas told me one day in conversation that he saw the car that did the South Braintree job going through Randolph very fast.

"When we started we went from Providence first to Boston and then back to Providence, and then back to South Braintree, getting there about noon. We spent some time in a speakeasy in South Braintree two or three miles from the place of the crime, leaving the car in the yard of the house. When we went to Boston we went to South Boston and stopped in Andrew Square. I stayed in the car. The others went into a saloon to get information, as they told me, about the money that was to be sent to South Braintree.[8]

"I had never been to South Braintree before. These four men persuaded me to go with them two or three nights before when I was talking with them in a saloon in Providence. The saloon was also a poolroom near my boarding house. They talked like professionals. They said they had done lots of jobs of this kind. They had been engaged in robbing freight cars in Providence. Two were young men from twenty to twenty-five years old, one was about forty, the other about thirty-five. All wore caps. I was then eighteen years old. I do not remember whether they were shaved or not. Two of them did the shooting—the oldest one and another. They were left on the street. The arrangement was that they should meet me in a Providence saloon the next night to divide the money. I went there but they did not come.

"I sat on the back seat of the automobile. I had a

[8] Madeiros was hazy as to the movements of the car after leaving Andrew Square until the exchange in Randolph woods.

Colt thirty-eight calibre automatic but did not use it. I was told that I was there to help hold back the crowd in case they made a rush. The curtains on the car were flapping. I do not remember whether there was any shotgun or rifle in the car or not.

"These men talked a lot about New York. As soon as I got enough money I went to New York and also to Chicago, hoping to find them in cabarets spending the money, but I never found them.

"They had been stealing silk, shoes, cotton, etc., from freight cars and sending it to New York. Two of them lived on South Main Street and two on North Main Street, in lodging houses.[9] I had known them three or four months. The old man was called Mike. Another one was called Williams or Bill. I don't remember what the others were called.[10]

"The money that they took from the men in South Braintree was in a black bag, I think.

"I was scared to death when I heard the shooting begin.

"Both cars had Massachusetts numbers.

"The names of these men don't amount to anything. They change them whenever they want to. When they are driven out of New York they come to Providence.

[9] Madeiros later admitted that these addresses were false.
[10] Madeiros later admitted that "the names of the men wasn't true;" that he knew the right names of the members of the gang but refused to tell.

I haven't any idea where they are now. I have never seen any of them since.

"Sacco and Vanzetti had nothing to do with this job, and neither did Gerald Chapman. It was entirely put up by the oldest of the Italians in Providence." [11]

As I told Mrs. Monterio the substance of the Madeiros story, her apparent doubt unexpectedly produced the first corroborative evidence of the investigation.

"Fred [Madeiros] couldn't have been it," she said when I finished. "I believe he was in Mexico at the time." I have never known whether Mrs. Monterio was seeking to protect Madeiros against himself or whether she was expressing her actual belief. From facts known to her she soon admitted that he must have left New Bedford on his southern travels about January, 1921. However, in her first effort to fix the time, Mrs. Monterio produced a package of letters which had been left in her custody by the former "bouncer." These letters again showed his criminal technique since their tops were torn off so that the finder could not ascertain the date or the place from which they were written. The letters were from a young lady who had traveled around with Madeiros and spoke of the presents he had given her and the

[11] The Madeiros account differs in two important particulars from the version of the prosecution: two cars were used in the escape instead of one; there was considerable delay in the Randolph woods instead of a continuous flight. These vital differences will be considered in a subsequent chapter.

good times they had enjoyed together. Apparently, he had spent considerable money on his travels.

"He told me all about his trip," continued Mrs. Monterio. "It must have been wonderful. First he went to Texas, then to Mexico, then to St. Paul, Minnesota, then back to Texas twice. It lasted for nearly two years. His friend was a circus girl."

"Did he tell you how much money he had when he started?"

"Yes—he said he took twenty-eight hundred dollars with him."

Twenty-eight hundred dollars! Where had Madeiros acquired such a large sum of money? Shortly after the South Braintree crime, Madeiros had been arrested, first on May 1, and again May 25, 1920. Prior to these arrests, he had been collecting small contributions for the American Rescue League— whatever that was. On June 14, 1920, he was found guilty of breaking and entering and committing larceny in the night-time. For this crime—which netted Madeiros only a trifling sum—he was sentenced to five months in the New Bedford House of Correction. There had been, therefore, scarcely any opportunity for Madeiros to accumulate twenty-eight hundred dollars and yet it was apparently waiting for him when he completed his sentence in December, 1920. I could not refrain from making a simple calculation. Fifteen thousand seven hundred and seventy-six dollars was the payroll stolen in South Braintree. According to

Madeiros there were six men involved. If divided equally, the loot would yield Madeiros about twenty-six hundred dollars.

Mrs. Monterio was most eager to see Madeiros. I promised to obtain an opportunity for her if she and her husband got in touch with me. On this visit I did not ask her for an affidavit or for the letters. What I wanted to establish was a basis of confidence so that Barney and his handsome wife would feel free to tell us everything they knew.

Ultimately my restraint was rewarded, because subsequently both the Monterios voluntarily went with me to Mr. Thompson's office. Mrs. Monterio saw Madeiros in the Dedham jail as she desired, and the interview was of considerable value. Her husband admitted that Madeiros had told him all about his participation in the South Braintree crime. Cautious Barney, however, ducked the vengeance of the guilty gang by claiming that Madeiros had never told him who his associates were. Like Madeiros, however, Barney, "off the record," knew who they were and put enough in his affidavit to identify the crowd. But this did not occur until long after the events narrated in the next chapter.

# CHAPTER THREE

# PAY-DIRT IN PROVIDENCE

TURNING SOUTH from Bluebird Inn I headed for police headquarters in Providence. As the distance from Seekonk was but a few miles across the state line I arrived at the dingy police station on Fountain Street late in the afternoon of the same day. The purpose of my visit was of vital importance, since a single unfavorable answer to my questions would prove Madeiros a liar and end the investigation. Affirmative answers, on the other hand, while not proving the truth of Madeiros' assertions, would at least dissipate the air of improbability which surrounded his statement.

I found Chief Inspector Connors on duty and he, an inspector in uniform, and another officer listened skeptically to my story. Their attitude of doubt was not disconcerting, however, since I shared it, and sought only the facts in their possession. Mr. Thompson had previously telephoned the Providence police and had received the encouraging word that they recalled a prosecution for freight-car thefts in that city.

44

The wire connection had been so poor, however, and the information so meager, that we were scarcely hopeful of finding facts which would at once confirm Madeiros and satisfy the known requirements of the case.

Chief Connors' response took us over the first great hurdle at a bound. In 1919 or 1920 there had been a group of criminals in Providence engaged in robbing freight cars; they were known as the "Morell gang" because a number of Morell brothers belonged to it.

"Were they Italians?" I interrupted anxiously.

"American-born Italians." We were over the second hurdle, but there was still a third.

"Were they at liberty on April 15, 1920?" The effort to answer this question kept me on the rack for half an hour. The officers sent for the police blotter which showed that Joseph, Frederick and Pasquale Morell had first been arrested on October 18, 1919. They then began to refresh one another's recollection by reference to various events and alternated between favorable and adverse opinions. Finally they fixed the trial in May, 1920, and concluded—correctly, as it proved—that most of the gang had been out on bail during the preceding month. The third hurdle was thus taken in a stride and the investigation was thenceforth to run without encountering a single impassable barrier. From now on it was possible to believe in Madeiros.

The information that the crime at South Braintree

had been committed on a day which fell between the indictment and the trial of the supposed bandits was of peculiar significance to me. During my investigation in Cleveland I had learned from veteran police detectives that a crook is never so dangerous as when he, or his pal, is facing trial for a serious offense. Money must be raised at such time in large amounts for lawyer's fees, bail bondsmen, and expenses. Facing a desperate situation in any event, the criminal has less to lose by risking another crime. The indicted gunman on bail is doubly a menace.

Chief Connors then referred me to various members of the local police force and others who could give me more direct information on the Morell brothers. Hereafter they will be referred to as Morelli, since this is the name by which they are generally known. Later I visited these officers and from some of them obtained interesting descriptions and views of the members of the "Morelli mob" but nothing bearing on the South Braintree murders. Nevertheless, those who knew the gang intimately showed no skepticism about the possibility of their committing the crime. Two names mentioned by Connors, however, opened up new and important lines of investigation. One was Captain Ralph Pieraccini of the police at New Bedford, Massachusetts, who, Connors thought, could tell about "Mike" and Frank Morelli in that city. The other was John J. Richards, a Providence

lawyer who had been United States Marshal at the
time of the Federal prosecution of the gang.

I left the Fountain Street Station in a mood of
great relief and telephoned to Mr. Thompson the
news that the Madeiros story still lived. He, too, I
am confident, had expected the trail to end almost at
its beginning, but it was contrary to his nature ever
to reveal discouragement to an associate. After tele-
phoning, I went to a restaurant and, in a secluded
corner, endeavored to arrange in my mind the information obtained during the day and to select the most
promising clues. This process was shortly completed,
and when the coffee and cigar arrived I was already
absorbed in the kind of speculation which is at once
the most thrilling and the most important part of any
investigation.

There were hundreds of manufacturing towns in
New England, I reflected, and yet South Braintree
had been selected. There were thousands of other factories, yet Slater and Morrill and Rice and Hutchins
had been marked for the attack—it was only by chance
that the Rice and Hutchins payroll had not been included in the delivery. The scene and movements of
the money had apparently been thoroughly "scouted"
by someone on behalf of the robbers. It followed,
therefore, that there must be in existence somewhere
a link binding the bandits to South Braintree, Rice
and Hutchins, or Slater and Morrill. It was the fact
that the shoe-worker, Sacco, in 1917, had been em-

ployed for a few days at the Rice and Hutchins shoe
factory, but this circumstance was too remote to have
any significance and it had not been urged. Except
for this incident, volunteered by Sacco and unknown to
the prosecution, the evidence produced against Sacco
and Vanzetti was totally lacking such a link. If any
connection could be discovered between the Morellis
and the South Braintree factories, the conclusion
would be irresistible that Madeiros was telling the
truth. The prosecution would have to admit that it
simply was not within the laws of chance that Madeiros could invent a story that implicated a Rhode
Island gang of criminals branded with knowledge
of the two South Braintree factories. Or so it seemed
to me on May 22, 1926, before the link was discovered.

I knew that the payroll robbery must have proceeded from inside information—a tip from some
employee—or from outside observation. If either
method could be brought home to the Morellis, the
case was made out. Pondering over "inside information," I had a flash that seemed like inspiration
at the time. "Slater and Morrill," I kept repeating to
myself, and then "Morrill, Morrell, Morrill, Morrell."
The sound was the same, the names were the same!
In an instant I saw the whole dramatic story. Morrill, of Slater and Morrill, was really an Italian, a
Morrell, a relative of the Providence family; he had
settled in Massachusetts, changed his name, and risen

to a position of affluence. The worthless Providence
Morrells had gotten into desperate straits on account
of the Federal indictments, had appealed to their rich
relative in South Braintree for aid, and been refused.
For money and revenge the gang had then robbed
their relative and murdered his payroll agents. It
was an exciting theory, but unfortunately did not last
out the next day. The South Braintree Morrill turned
out to be an elderly gentleman, recently deceased, of
eminently respectable Yankee lineage, always "Morrill" in the male line. My disappointment over this
blind alley was soon dispelled, however, by the discovery of the true road from Providence to Braintree.
It followed the false by a few hours and came in a
form, if less romantic, yet more in accord with the
habits of professional criminals.

Three nights later I was again in Providence, at the
home of Daniel E. Geary, the lawyer who had defended the Morellis at the trial on the Federal indictments. Mr. Geary appreciated the serious purpose
of my visit, but also felt his professional duty toward
his former clients. He was unwilling to disclose matters learned by him in a confidential way and asked
to be excused from becoming a witness or an affiant
in the case. He stood ready, however, to help us in
obtaining information which had become public during the trial and I asked his assistance in this respect.
Fortunately for the investigation, the Assistant District Attorney in Massachusetts at a later date at-

tempted to quote Mr. Geary as to movements of the
Morellis in April, 1920, and Mr. Geary was put into
a position where he could not refuse our request for
a counter-affidavit setting forth his version of the facts.
Important as this affidavit proved to be, it omitted
one significant statement made to me for the reason
that Mr. Geary could not confirm his recollection by
any record of the trial.

The main point of my inquiries was to ascertain
how the Morellis had received information of the shipments of merchandise later stolen by them in freight
yards of Providence. It was obvious that they had
not indulged in haphazard theft since their larcenies
were almost entirely of shoes and textiles and were
uniformly disposed of through "fences" engaged in
the retail sale of these commodities. Mr. Geary stated
that the principal method used was by "spotting"
shipments, which meant that the gang posted one of
their number to watch the factories and railroad stations in the manufacturing towns. The "spotter" would
watch the shipment being made and get the number
of the freight car into which it was placed. This would
enable the gang to "crack" the car when it arrived
in the Providence yards without risking time and apprehension involved in an ignorant rifling of the train.
They did not overlook anything additional, however,
which might be in the car.

I asked Mr. Geary how he knew the spotting method
had been used. He replied that one of the railroad

detectives had stated that Joe Morelli, at an early
time when evidence was being gathered against the
gang, had boldly taken him to various places and
showed him where the shipments were spotted. This,
Geary thought, was a ruse by Joe, the gang leader,
to divert suspicion from himself. When I asked Mr.
Geary if he recalled any particular place, his reply
sent the blood pounding to my head.

"Well, I remember one place, the Rice and Hutchins shoe factory." This was said without any apparent
appreciation of its significance.

"Rice and Hutchins!" I exclaimed. "That's in
South Braintree, where the murders occurred!"

Mr. Geary gave a low whistle and then observed,
"That brings it home, doesn't it!" His trained mind
had perceived instantly the link between the Providence gang and the South Braintree crime. But
the spontaneous mention of Rice and Hutchins, the
whistle and the observation never got into Mr. Geary's
affidavit. He made a diligent search for the portion of
the trial record containing the testimony of the railroad detective and failed to locate it. The only report he could use for checking his recollection was
a contemporaneous newspaper summary of the testimony and Mr. Geary adopted its language as the more
conservative course. Instead of "Rice and Hutchins,"
therefore, the affidavit subsequently recited, "Taunton, Attleboro, and other places in Massachusetts."
We sought the court stenographer who had taken this

portion of the Morelli trial and located her in Florida. Her memory was the same as that of Mr. Geary, but her notes had disappeared. Later the railroad detective gave to the Assistant District Attorney an affidavit in which he denied having gone to South Braintree with Joe Morelli or having so stated. He was silent, however, as to Mr. Geary's allegation in regard to his visiting other towns in that section of Massachusetts in the company of Joe Morelli to inspect places where shipments had been "spotted" and the District Attorney conceded that this was true.

Meanwhile a record fact had appeared which dwarfed the importance of Mr. Geary's first recollection and rendered necessary only his statement as to the method of "spotting" shipments. That this was the means employed was subsequently confirmed by Mr. Richards, the United States Marshal whose thorough preparation of the Federal case against the Morellis had resulted in their conviction. It was never questioned by anyone throughout our investigation. I left Mr. Geary's home, my head buzzing with the significance of "spotting" shipments and the casual remark about Rice and Hutchins, to meet Mrs. Ehrmann at the Providence-Biltmore Hotel. I had asked her to take a look at the Federal indictments of the Morellis in the clerk's office of the United States District Court. This was a routine matter which had to be done and I was glad to have her assistance. It had left me free during that afternoon to run down various potential clues.

Mrs. Ehrmann was blazing with excitement when she met me in the lobby of the hotel. She had made some notes of the indictments from the court dockets and when she handed the paper to me, I realized that my interview with Mr. Geary had been merely preparatory to the indisputable evidence which she had seen. This is what I read:

| | |
|---|---|
| Indictment<br>No. 563 | United States<br>v.<br>Joseph Morelli et als. |
| First Count | " . . . two hundred and twenty-eight pairs of ladies shoes from *Rice and Hutchins, at South Braintree in the Commonwealth of Massachusetts. . . .* " |
| Second Count | " . . . one hundred and fifty-one pairs of ladies shoes from *Rice and Hutchins, at South Braintree, in the Commonwealth of Massachusetts. . . .* " |
| Third Count | " . . . one hundred and twenty-seven pairs of ladies shoes from *Rice and Hutchins, at South Braintree, in the Commonwealth of Massachusetts. . . .* " |
| Fourth Count | " . . . one hundred and five pairs of ladies shoes from *Rice and Hutchins at South Braintree, in the Commonwealth of Massachusetts. . . .* " |
| Eighth Count | " . . . seventy-eight pairs of men's shoes, from *Slater and Morrill, Inc., at South Braintree, in the Commonwealth of Massachusetts. . . .* " |

The link was forged. The record of the conviction of the Morellis on this indictment seemed to carry with it the irresistible inference of complete knowledge necessary to plan the payroll crime. The station in South Braintree where the money arrived by express in the morning, the building opposite to which it was taken to be sorted, the walk of a few hundred yards by the paymaster and his guard to deliver their precious box—all this would be known in detail by the gangster carefully watching and checking shipments. Madeiros could not be lying, because only a miracle of chance could so favor a liar, and such miracles did not happen. I felt sure that this startling confirmation of Madeiros would cause the District Attorney's office to take up the investigation and replace our amateurish efforts with the authority and facilities of Massachusetts. At any rate, I felt that night that if not another piece of evidence were discovered, the Commonwealth could not destroy Sacco and Vanzetti with this ineradicable fact in the record. I was badly mistaken.

# CHAPTER FOUR

# SERGEANT JACOBS' NOTEBOOK

OUT OF Providence, the trail led to New Bedford, Massachusetts, where Chief Connors had suggested I would learn more about Frank and Mike Morelli. Frank lived in Providence but had frequented New Bedford where Mike lived. I expected also to pick up a few facts concerning the earlier history of Madeiros, whose home had been in New Bedford. On the whole, the trip had a routine purpose, and I so explained it to the friend who accompanied me. However, to understand the full meaning of the information unexpectedly revealed in New Bedford, it is necessary to revert to a feature of the South Braintree crime.

On the road from Boston to New Bedford one passes through the Bridgewaters, a section replete with memories of the Sacco-Vanzetti case.[1] Of immediate inter-

---

[1] It was at Bridgewater on December 24, 1919, that the attempted payroll robbery occurred for which Vanzetti was convicted shortly after his arrest. It was Bridgewater's Chief of Police, Michael Stewart, engaged in tracking Reds for the Department of Justice, who first conceived the idea that this crime was the work of radicals and set the trap at the West Bridgewater garage for the owners of the old Over-

est to us is the wild and heavily wooded region near the village of Cochesett, known as the Manley woods. Here on April 17, 1920, there had been found an abandoned seven-passenger Buick touring car, 1920 model, closely resembling the murder car which had sped out of South Braintree with the bandits and the money.[2] The car was later identified by its owner as one purchased by him in September, 1919, and stolen from him on November 23, 1919. When found, the rear window was out and the curtains were arranged as in the murder car.[3] Alongside of the tracks left in the sandy soil by the Buick were the tracks of smaller

land car mentioned in the preface to this book. When, in the summer of 1920, the District Attorney took the preparation of the Sacco-Vanzetti case out of the hands of the veteran Captain Proctor, head of the State police, he entrusted the work to this town police officer of Bridgewater.

[2] The spot where the Buick was found was only 1.8 miles from the place where the prosecution alleged it had been kept, a garage adjoining the house of Coacci, the deported radical, and Boda, the owner of the ancient Overland. It apparently did not impress the prosecution as peculiar that murderers and robbers should plant such striking evidence in their own neighborhood. However, the state also claimed that Vanzetti's revolver had once belonged to the murdered Berardelli and that for over four months he had carried around several shotgun shells of a type alleged to have been discharged at the Bridgewater attempt. Such feeble-mindedness on the part of the criminals was not evident in the perfect planning and execution of the crime itself. What Captain Proctor thought of these various claims will never be known since he died after revealing some disgust and disbelief in the case.

[3] When this car was presented to the jury there was a bullet hole through the right rear door, although a careful examination of the car in the Manley woods by several persons failed to discover such a tell-tale mark. This type of corroborative detail, apparently supplied by

tires. The car had some dust on it. It was the Government theory at the trial that the criminals had made a continuous flight in the Buick for about twenty miles to the Manley woods and there changed to another car.

Madeiros, however, maintained that he and the other bandits had left Providence in a Hudson touring car, but had switched to a Buick in the Oak Street woods in Randolph, about three and a half miles from South Braintree. "We went from Providence to Randolph, where we changed to a Buick car brought there by another Italian. We left the Hudson car in the woods and took it again after we did the job, leaving the Buick in the woods in charge of one man who drove it off to another part of the woods, as I understood." He later explained that two, and sometimes three cars are customarily used on jobs of this kind and that the purpose of exchanging cars is to avoid recognition. Then, "One or two cars is thrown away at night—left somewhere, thrown into a pond or deserted."

In a later chapter the theory of continuous flight in the Buick will be contrasted with Madeiros' description of a prompt exchange. The Madeiros story, however, introduces a new member of the gang, an Italian who procured a Buick car, brought it to the rendezvous in the Oak Street woods, drove it off following

the police in charge, prepared the minds of Mr. Thompson and myself to doubt the more vital exhibits in the case, such as the so-called mortal bullet and shell.

the exchange after the crime, and then threw it away at night. This individual was not in my mind as we skirted Cochesett on our way to New Bedford, but I was soon to suspect his identity. I did, however, observe that after leaving the Bridgewaters one rolls rather easily for about twenty-five miles to New Bedford, the single interruption to a constant rural scene being the town of Middleboro. The mills of New Bedford with their hum of activity present a striking contrast to the quiet of lake and countryside through which one approaches that textile center.

Arriving at police headquarters we inquired immediately for Captain Pieraccini and found him in his office. He listened politely to my request for information in regard to Mike Morelli, but when I mentioned the story of Madeiros and Sacco and Vanzetti his eyes snapped with a sudden interest. He interrupted my narrative.

"We'd better have Jake in," he said simply and sent for Jake. Presently Sergeant Ellsworth C. Jacobs of the New Bedford police bulked into the room.

"Listen to this, Jake," said Pieraccini. So I told again the story of the Madeiros confession. The big sergeant also interrupted me.

"Let me show you my 1920 notebook," he said and wheeled out of the room.

"He's gone to his locker," commented Pieraccini. "You'll see something." And we did.

Sergeant Jacobs returned with an old and much-used pocket notebook. He first showed us an entry in pencil, undated, which read, "R. I. 154 E, Buick touring car, Mike Morrell."

"That means," explained Sergeant Jacobs, "that one evening I saw Mike Morell driving what looked like a new Buick touring car. He was with two other men. I knew Mike and suspected that he had stolen the car or was up to some mischief. So I wrote down the number-plate figure."

"When was this?" I asked.

"Well, from the next entry in my book, it must have been a few days before April 15, because on that date I saw the car again, with the same number, and jotted it down." There it was, in pencil, "154 E, April 15."

"It was in the afternoon," continued Jacobs, "and I caught the rear end of the car as it passed me going by the post office. I did not see who was in it on this occasion, but made a note of the number which I recognized."

"Can you fix the time of day?" This was a critical question because an early hour of the afternoon would rule out Mike and the Buick. Sergeant Jacobs thought out loud.

"I was an inspector then with Ralph here [Pieraccini] and was on my way to report at police headquarters where I was due at five-thirty o'clock. It is seven or eight minutes' walk from the post office to police headquarters. But then I may have been a bit early as I often was. I should say it was between five and five-thirty o'clock."

Click! Mike Morelli was in the picture. This member of the gang was landed with the possession of a Buick automobile of the same type and age as the murder car at precisely the critical time. Moreover, this Buick vanished after April 15, 1920. Why? My mind reverted to the scrub oak in the Randolph woods and I could see Mike Morelli, the New Bedford brother, bringing the Buick to the meeting-place. I could picture the hasty return of the Buick from South Braintree, the switching of the money boxes and number-plates, and then Mike Morelli's leisurely and unsuspected drive from Randolph to New Bedford. Under cover of night the pleasant roll to the Manley woods would be accomplished with another car trailing to take Mike away from the abandoned evidence of his complicity.

But Sergeant Jacobs had not completed his narrative. He referred again to his notebook, indicating an entry dated May 24, 1920, "154 E. Black Cole '8' Touring." He then related the following incident while my friend and I listened like children to a ghost story.

"On the afternoon of April 24, I found a big, black, dull-looking touring car, a Cole '8', standing at the curb in front of Joe Fiore's restaurant at the corner of Kempton and Purchase Streets. What attracted my attention especially about the Cole car was the num-

ber plate, "R. I. 154 E." It was the same number I
had seen on the new Buick, the one that Mike Morell
had been driving. The whole thing looked fishy, so I
went into the restaurant to inquire, although I was not
on duty at the time. At a table inside I saw four men
who looked like Italians, one of whom was Frank
Morell, a brother of Mike, from Providence, but a fre-
quent visitor at New Bedford.

"The men at the table were extremely nervous
when they saw me come in. I can't say just what it
was, but they acted apprehensive of something. One
of the Italians whom I remember distinctly was a short
heavy-set man with a wide, square face, high cheek
bones, smooth shaven and dark brown hair. He was
about thirty-five to forty years of age and, judging
from his appearance as he sat at the table, I should
say he was about five feet six or seven inches in height
and weighed about one hundred and seventy pounds.
I can never forget that man's face. As I approached
the group, this man made a movement with his hand
toward his pocket and I thought he was going to
draw a gun. As I was unarmed at the time I was badly
scared, but tried not to show it. Fortunately, Frank
spoke up and relieved the situation somewhat.

" 'What's the matter, Jake?' he said quickly. 'What
do you want with me? Why are you picking on me
all the time?' "

" 'Look here, Frank,' I said 'there's a Cole car
downstairs with a number-plate that I've seen on a

Buick car that Mike's been driving. How did that happen?'

"At that the bunch eased up somewhat.

" 'Oh,' said Frank, 'that's a dealer's plate. You see, I'm in the automobile business and we just transfer plates from one car to another.' "

"At the time I had no way of contradicting Frank, so I left the restaurant and talked the matter over later with Ralph. At the time of the South Braintree murders and payroll robbery he and I had suspected the Morells, especially on account of Mike and the Buick car, so that the actions of that bunch at Fiore's made us more suspicious. Shortly after that, however, Sacco and Vanzetti were arrested and as I had no definite evidence, I dropped the matter. I never saw Frank again since approximately that time, but Mike hung around New Bedford for possibly a year afterward."

In this manner did Sergeant Jacobs throw the web of circumstances around the Morellis, with Captain Pieraccini nodding his approval. Astonishment is the only word descriptive of my emotion. Only a few days before I had set out for the Bluebird Inn feeling that Madeiros had invented an impossible story. Confirmation had accumulated with great rapidity and in uncontrovertible form, but I was totally unprepared for the news that police officials of New Bedford, in April, 1920, had suspected, with good reason, the very gang implicated by Madeiros.

Hurriedly I appraised the importance of Sergeant

Jacobs' story. The appearance of the new Buick just
before April 15, with Mike Morelli driving, its second
appearance late in the afternoon of April 15, and its
dropping from view thereafter led to the vital inferences already mentioned. The worn pocket notebook
with its pencil-scrawled numerals and dates riveted
the events to the fatal day. When the number-plate,
"R. I. 154 E," had been transferred from the Buick
to the Cole 8, the gap to the gang in Providence had
been closed because the Cole car was notoriously the
gang vehicle in Providence.[4] The Buick was therefore
linked not merely to Mike but to the entire mob.

The actions of the men in Fiore's restaurant plainly
indicated consciousness of having done something
pretty serious. The nervousness and apprehension at
the sight of Jacobs and the movement by the stranger
as if to draw a weapon might have produced a conflict
had not Frank Morelli's words broken the tension with
their note of familiarity. What had these men to fear
from Jacobs? Why did Frank Morelli lie about being
in the automobile business? Actually he had no known
occupation except that of gambling. What was he trying to conceal in connection with the transfer of the
number-plate? A few days after my visit to New Bedford this same Frank Morelli was interviewed by the

---

[4] The Cole 8 was the property of Joe Morelli, and was used by the
gang for various purposes including the spotting of shipments. It was
mentioned by Mr. Geary, Marshal Richards and later by Madeiros
in his deposition.

Massachusetts District Attorney, Mr. Wilbar, and told that official that he had "been in Providence the entire month of April, 1920." Yet Frank's presence in New Bedford at the time was affirmed by his own lawyer, Mr. Geary, and by the Marshal, Mr. Richards, and by his own testimony at his trial on the Federal indictments given in May, 1920. Why did Frank lie to Mr. Wilbar, who was questioning him in regard to the South Braintree crime and the Madeiros confession? In the light of the evidence which had already been uncovered, I thought that the only inference possible from such conduct was the one drawn by the New Bedford police in April, 1920.

There was a special reason why I believed that the inference of guilt would be drawn. Judge Webster Thayer, who had presided over the trial of Sacco and Vanzetti, had stated in one of his decisions that what convicted them was evidence indicating "consciousness of guilt." This evidence consisted mainly of lies told by them when taken into custody and alleged movements which the arresting officer thought were for the purpose of drawing weapons.[5] But Sacco and Vanzetti were admittedly radicals and draft-dodgers whose comrades were being hounded by the agents of the Department of Justice and, as they believed with some

[5] The arresting officer made no mention of these alleged movements when testifying to the same arrest at the trial of Vanzetti in 1920, but a year later, at the trial of Sacco and Vanzetti, he gave a graphic recital which was contradicted by the defendants.

reason, even tortured and killed. Whether or not the jury believed the explanation of Sacco and Vanzetti, it rested on a sound psychological basis. Moreover, they were foreign-born immigrants, speaking little English and understanding it with difficulty, naturally fearful of strange institutions. The Morellis, on the other hand, were American-born and "sophisticated" to an extreme. They were neither furtive radicals nor "cop-shy" immigrants to be thrown into confusion upon the approach of a policeman. I was confident that the doctrine of "consciousness of guilt," so fatal to Sacco and Vanzetti, would be applied with even more crushing effect to the Morellis.

A preliminary test came much sooner than I had expected. We returned that afternoon from New Bedford after gathering considerable additional data concerning the Morellis and Madeiros. Whether it was that same night, or a few days later after a second trip to New Bedford, I do not now remember, but on one of those evenings I had occasion to telephone to the Assistant District Attorney then in charge of the Sacco-Vanzetti case.[6] He had been a classmate of mine at college and I felt that I could talk frankly to him. To my surprise he showed no interest whatsoever in the news from New Bedford and Providence. I concluded my narrative by suggesting that the investigation of the Madeiros story would probably end by his

[6] Dudley P. Ranney, Esq. He had not been connected in any way with the trial of Sacco and Vanzetti, but came into the case years later.

nol-prossing (dismissal by prosecuting officer) the cases against Sacco and Vanzetti. The sudden hostility of his tone and the finality of his reply sent me away from the telephone flushed, angry and disillusioned. For the first time a fear began to come over me that perhaps the usual rules of the game were not to be applied to Nicola Sacco and Bartolomeo Vanzetti.

CHAPTER FIVE

# ASSEMBLING
# THE MURDER PARTY

WE NOW felt that the Morelli gang was firmly
linked to the outrage in South Braintree. The confession of a confederate had led to the discovery of circumstantial evidence more important, as proof, than
the story itself. The arm of coincidence could not possibly have been long enough to corroborate a manufactured story by producing the requisite gang,
spreading on the records of the Federal Court their
connection with the Slater and Morrill and the Rice
and Hutchins factories, writing in Sergeant Jacobs'
notebook the adventure of the timely Buick and the
episode in Fiore's restaurant. Nevertheless, the official
attitude in Massachusetts continued not merely apa-
thetic but hostile toward the new evidence. We continued, therefore, to carry the burden of a private
investigation in order to establish further, if possible,
the identity of each individual member of the murder
party.

Mr. Thompson had already carried the investigation
to the State prison at Charlestown where a close friend

67

of Madeiros was serving a life sentence for accompanying him on the Wrentham Bank venture. Jimmie Weeks was a mild, soft-spoken young man, not much older than Madeiros. Prior to the fatal expedition to the Wrentham National Bank his most serious known offense had been the theft of automobiles. Of Yankee lineage, some education and obvious refinement, a trained electrician, Weeks presented to the criminologist a more difficult problem than did his eccentric companion in crime. Whatever weakness of character may have brought him low, however, he was now about to display unusual moral courage.

When first visited by Mr. Thompson on May 21, 1926, Jimmie refused to talk. Mr. Thompson then appealed to Mr. Hoggsett, the deputy warden,[1] who, in turn, urged Weeks to tell the truth. Several days later, Mr. Thompson received a message which resulted in the first interview on May 25. Mr. Thompson then learned that Madeiros had frequently discussed his part in the South Braintree crime with Weeks and had planned the Wrentham robbery along the same lines.[2] Even more important, however, was Weeks' statement detailing the individual members of the

[1] Now warden of the prison.
[2] In the Wrentham job, Madeiros had used two stolen cars, a Hudson and a Buick; the rear glass had been removed and a shotgun carried to cover any pursuit; prior to the crime they had even gone to the same saloon in South Boston which Madeiros claimed had been visited in the early hours of April 15, 1920, to obtain information about the payroll.

Morelli gang participating in the crime as related to him by Madeiros. This gave us the starting point in reconstructing the murder party. He concluded by stating, "It is well known and has long been well known among a certain crowd who did that job."

Scarcely had Mr. Thompson left in order to prepare an affidavit, than Weeks was visited by an Assistant District Attorney [3] and a State detective. The occasion for this call was the erroneous report that Weeks had confessed his own complicity in the South Braintree crime. To these gentlemen Weeks confirmed his statements to Mr. Thompson. He stated afterward, however, that they had tried to influence him against signing any statement by threatening to indict him for the South Braintree and other offenses, and by discussing his chances for commutation. Any efforts to frighten Weeks out of giving an affidavit were denied, however, and the notes taken by a police stenographer at the interview were produced. Even from these notes, however, it appears that Weeks' chances for commutation were discussed, and that he was told, "Anyone that comes here to see you and wants information, you have to look out for yourself." Instead of declining to sign a statement, Jimmie told the story to Mr. Hoggsett and later gave a much fuller interview to Mr. Thompson.[4]

[3] Not Mr. Ranney.
[4] Strangely enough, Weeks reports that after the execution of Sacco and Vanzetti in 1927, he continued to receive visits from State detectives urging him to retract his story, the last being in 1930.

From many other sources information was received concerning the Morelli gang and its members. I paid a routine call on John J. Richards, the Providence lawyer who had been United States Marshal at the time of the Federal prosecution of the Morellis. Mr. Richards instantly became interested in my story and soon became active in the investigation, even accompanying me to the Leavenworth penitentiary in Kansas, where Joe Morelli was doing his "stretch." Through the eyes of Mr. Richards, we were able to see the members of the crowd in their natural colors. As United States Marshal he had prepared the evidence on the freight-car robbery charges, and his views were all close-ups. Danger and adventure seemed to have a peculiar appeal for him. As a youth he had stoked furnaces on tramp steamers sailing the tropics. The Spanish-American War had called him. As United States Marshal, he took personal charge of criminal cases. At night, in the freight yards, he had used his pistol on the Morelli shadows who fired

The same State detective who saw Weeks in 1926 also interviewed Miller, the runner in the Dedham jail, concerning the delivery of the Madeiros confession. When Miller's recollection did not accord with that of Mr. Curtis, this detective began to talk about Miller's prospects of getting out. Miller then exclaimed that he could see they were going to jail him on a suspended sentence when he got out. Miller declined to change his story, but when his term at Dedham expired, his prophecies proved correct.

During 1927, before the decision of the Governor was announced, Weeks had received another visitor seeking a retraction. This individual was a resident of Providence, Rhode Island, and represented himself as acting for the Morellis.

THE MURDER PARTY 71

at him as they fled; in the daytime, when proximity and occasion permitted, he used his foot on their more substantial presence. His older partner confided to me that "Jack was a fool for danger. Why, when he was Marshal, I barely prevented him from accepting Joe Morelli's invitation to visit that criminal's home at midnight in the hope of obtaining evidence." If Mr. Richards' partner reads this, he will learn for the first time that Jack did not follow his advice, but sat for over an hour in a little room adjoining Joe's kitchen, with blinds drawn and pistol ready, waiting for something which never happened. In appearance, the former Marshal looked the soldier of fortune— powerful physique, blond mustache, high color, gray eyes, and authoritative carriage so different from the deprecating attitude of the mere lawyer.

From the stories of Weeks, Richards and the Providence authorities, the records of jails, courts and police, we were able to begin our tentative assignment of the actual individuals who invaded South Braintree with such fatal results. As Mike Morelli was much younger than Joe, the boss of the gang, it was obvious that Madeiros had endeavored to mislead us when he gave the name of Mike to the "oldest of the Italians" who planned the job. Madeiros himself said to Mr. Thompson that he was trying to "shield a gang" and to Mr. Ranney that "the names aren't true." When arrested, Madeiros had used the same device for confusing the police in calling himself "Bedard", which was the name of one of his accomplices in the Wrentham crime.[5] It seemed safer to begin with the list of participants as told to Weeks by Madeiros in the carefree days before either was a prisoner.

The Morelli brothers consisted of Joe, the oldest; Frank, nicknamed "Butsy"; Michael, known as "Mike"; Pasquale, or "Patsy"; and Fred. The names of the associates of Madeiros as given to Weeks were "Mike," "Joe," "Bill" and "Butsy." He had, therefore, identified three of the Morelli brothers by name, Joseph the oldest, Michael of New Bedford, and Frank. "Bill" was marked as not being a Morelli brother, for Weeks further stated that Madeiros did not mention "Patsy" as being on the job, nor was there any reference to Fred's name.[6] As a matter of fact, Fred was in jail at the time and so could not have participated. The identity of "Bill" will be later considered.

"It was entirely put up by the oldest of the Italians," Madeiros had stated, estimating the leader's age at about forty years. Records of the Providence police showed that Joe was thirty-eight years old in October, 1919. Moreover, Joe was, beyond question,

[5] We also learned that the Morelli brothers assumed each other's first names on occasion. This information was not presented in affidavit form, however.

[6] Patsy and Fred were the two youngest brothers. Weeks erroneously stated to Mr. Thompson that Fred was known as Butsy, but his mistake was soon discovered and corrected. The evidence that Frank was Butsy was conclusive, and Mr. Ranney, the prosecutor in charge, conceded this to be the fact.

the boss of the gang and was reluctantly admitted by
Madeiros himself to be older than Mike. A more important question was whether Joe was capable of
planning and directing the details of the South Braintree robbery. We soon found that Joe's outstanding
quality was executive ability in the criminal field.
The highly organized scheme for robbing the freight
cars was alone a sufficient tribute to Joe. From the
spotting of the shipments at the point of origination
to the last step in making a safe delivery to the
"fence," the operation required careful planning and
the assignment of every active member to his post.
Property worth many thousands of dollars was stolen
in this manner, and so boldly and skillfully was the
work managed that the thefts continued for some
weeks during the period when members of the gang
were out on bail after their first arrest.

Although it was universally conceded that Joe
qualified as the man to plan the crime, some question
arose at first concerning his active participation in it.
This slight doubt arose from the fact that Joe apparently ignored the code of the gangster—he protected
nobody and he blamed everybody. At his own trial in
Providence, where he was found to be the brains of
the gang, he attempted to "throw" his own brothers
in order to escape conviction. Sentenced originally
to the Atlanta penitentiary by the Federal Court
at Providence, he was moved from institution to institution until in 1926 he had arrived at Leavenworth,

Kansas. This journey, it was reported, was brought about by Joe's habit of scheming with the other prisoners, turning his associates over to the authorities, and then being transferred beyond their vengeance, but with a letter of commendation from each former warden. Madeiros himself told Mr. Thompson that Joe would not admit his own guilt, but would blame the crime on his brothers. Another source of skepticism was the fact that Joe was boastful. He assured Mr. Richards, for instance, that stealing from freight trains was beneath his dignity, but that if it was a bank robbery or a "stick-up" job, that was more in his line. He was a "high class man." Returning from a sojourn of several years in New York, where he had been a fugitive from Rhode Island justice, Joe aroused the envy of his associates by claiming that he was wanted in the celebrated Rosenthal murder case.

However, those who knew Joe well did not doubt that he would be a principal actor at the South Braintree tragedy. Previously, he had shot a deputy sheriff and was saved from being a murderer at that time merely by defective aim. During and after his trial, he threatened the life of the marshal. On the instruction of the trial judge, he was searched in the courtroom. Neither the lawyer who defended him nor the marshal who prosecuted him expressed any doubts about his qualifications. Joe's capacity for murder was confirmed to me by the man who knew him best, who had every reason to maintain Joe's innocence because his own guilt was involved—Tony Mancini.

Madeiros' implication of Joe was confirmed by other facts. One of the bullets presented at the trial as having been extracted from the body of Berardelli, had been fired through a thirty-two calibre Colt automatic. It appeared that Joe Morelli had several such weapons. A witness at the trial, a railroad gate-tender along the route of escape, had testified that one of the bandits had yelled at him, "What in hell are you holding us up for!"—in English that was "unmistakable and clear." This robber was claimed to be Vanzetti, who could scarcely speak any English at all at that time. The brow-beating spirit, however, as well as the enunciation seemed more consonant with the theory that it was the American-born Joe Morelli. But our most startling confirmation, as will be seen later, occurred when we showed a rogue's gallery picture of Joe to some of the eye-witnesses to the shooting.

Frank Morelli, or "Butsy," certainly qualified for the job. He was generally regarded as the most dangerous of the brothers. During his trial he had threatened to kill his associate, Joe Imondi, and one of the fences who turned State's evidence told me he was in constant terror for fear of Frank. This brother later figured in a stabbing affray. He was a bird of passage, shifting about among Providence, New Bedford, and New York. Sergeant Jacobs has already described Frank's guilty actions in Joe

Fiore's restaurant at New Bedford. As Frank had sur-
rendered himself directly to the Federal authorities,
we could procure no rogue's gallery likeness from
the Providence police.

Mike Morelli had already been tied into the crime
by Sergeant Jacobs of New Bedford. Shortly before
the killing, Mike appeared in possession of a Buick
which corresponded to the one seen escaping from
South Braintree. This car vanished after April 15,
but the number-plate was transferred to Joe Morelli's
Cole 8. Mike was regarded by detectives in automobile insurance circles as an astute car thief, but I
could not get this opinion into affidavit form. To him
was assigned the task of bringing the Buick to the
Randolph woods, then guarding the Hudson while the
crime was being committed in South Braintree, and
disposing of the Buick unobtrusively after the robbery.

Madeiros himself was another member of the party.
At the scene of the crime he placed himself on the
rear seat of the Buick, behind the curtains. The District Attorney had referred in his opening to a bandit
as the "man we cannot describe in the back seat."

We now had placed three suspects in the murder
car and one on guard in the Randolph woods. The
two missing were the driver of the car and the murderer designated by Madeiros as "Bill." The chauffeur could not have been another Morelli, since by the
overwhelming testimony of witnesses, this individual

was pale and blond, whereas the brothers were dark-complexioned men. Nor, as has been seen, could Bill have been a Morelli, since Fred was in jail and Pasquale was a young man, whereas Bill was described as being the thirty-five-year-old bandit who did the shooting. It therefore became necessary to look for other available members of the gang to make a tentative assignment of the blond driver and the dark killer.

Candidates for the vacant seats in the murder car were Albert ("Bibba") Barone, Paul ("Pauli") Rossi, Joseph ("Gyp the Blood") Imondi, Raymond ("Ray") McDevitt, and Anthony ("Tony") Mancini.

At first the "Bibba" looked a likely prospect. His record as a convicted highwayman and his reputation for committing murderous assaults well fitted him to be Joe's companion on the streets of South Braintree. It was the Bibba whom Madeiros had outfaced on the porch before the Bluebird Inn when Barone's crowd had come to carry off a girl named Tessie.

"You and your gang have double-crossed me once on a job," Madeiros had shouted, gun in hand. "I might forgive you for that, but if you try to take this girl, I'll bump you all off!" [7]

[7] We never knew just what Madeiros meant by claiming that Barone's gang had "double-crossed" him. Weeks understood him to mean that the Morellis had not given him any share of the South Braintree loot whereas Barney Monterio believed that Madeiros felt he had not been paid his full share. Madeiros himself first claimed that he had not received his split, but on being examined by Mr. Thompson concerning the source of the money which he took south with him, declined to answer for fear "it might be traced back into the hands of these

The Bibba knew that Madeiros, the Bouncer, was rather handy with a gun and apparently decided that Tessie was not worth the duel. So far as the South Braintree crime was concerned, however, we had to discard Barone as a possible participant because we soon discovered that he had the perfect alibi—jail.

"Pauli" Rossi was apparently at liberty on April 15, 1920, and was bad enough to qualify, but was eliminated as a prospect after investigation. I do not now recall clearly why we dropped Pauli, but to the best of my recollection it came on the suggestion of Mr. Richards who had, I believed, questioned him in some Rhode Island jail where Rossi was temporarily detained.

Joe Imondi was also at large on the day of the murder, but was disqualified by disposition. He was known as a peaceable gangster, the tool, often unwillingly, of Joe Morelli, who had ironically christened him "Gyp the Blood," in derision and not in tribute. Gyp it was who entered the marked freight cars at

Italians." Barney's understanding appears confirmed not only by the money which seemed to have been awaiting Madeiros at the end of 1920, but by Madeiros' statement on examination that before the robbery in Providence he had been told that there would be four to five thousand dollars apiece in the job. He went south with twenty-eight hundred dollars. If the Rice and Hutchins payroll had been bagged at the same time by the bandits, their estimate of five thousand dollars each would not have been wide of the mark. Still another explanation may be that the gang failed to give him his "split" until he threatened trouble. This would reconcile his arrest in May, 1920, for rather petty thievery with his emergence from jail a few months later in possession of a huge "roll."

night by prying the lock with a brake-pin and who rolled out the boxes from the moving train for Joe to collect in the Cole 8 or truck when the coast was clear. The gang leaders apparently regarded Gyp as a good mechanic but not fitted for important work. When I asked the police about him in the summer of 1926, I learned that he was "going straight," which, on further inquiry, seemed to mean occasional boot-legging. At any rate, Gyp was too dark to have been the driver of the murder car, and temperamentally unfitted for the place of Bill, the killer.

"Ray" McDevitt was a light-complexioned young man, slender and rather good-looking. He was a thief, a hi-jacker and a hold-up man. In fact, Ray was killed during an attempted robbery in North Kingston, Rhode Island. He was not definitely a member of the Morelli gang, but hailed from their hangout in Paw-tucket and was engaged in freight-car robberies. He corresponded in general appearance to the driver of the car and was at liberty on April 15, 1920. Accord-ingly, we provisionally nominated him for the job. His picture, however, was never selected by any wit-nesses to whom we showed a group of photographs. This, in itself, would not have necessitated his im-mediate elimination, since the picture was merely a newspaper cut, full view only and such identification is not an easy task. It was the attitude of Madeiros which indicated clearly that we were making a mis-take. At first Madeiros had been content to have us

assume that the driver was an Italian like the others,
but on cross-examination by Mr. Thompson he had
admitted that this person was "Polish or Finland, or
something northern Europe." He then described the
slim blond chap substantially as witnesses had done,
except that Madeiros refused to concede a "sickly"
appearance. The "give-away" on McDevitt came when
Mr. Thompson was showing Madeiros pictures of
members of the Morelli gang. One after another of
these photographs was shown to him with the question,
"Have you ever seen the original of this picture?"
Always Madeiros had promptly made the same response, "I refuse to say." When the picture of Mc-
Devitt was shown him, Madeiros started off "Well,"
then hesitated a long time, then smiled and repeated
the formula, "I refuse to say." His action had told me
plainly that McDevitt had nothing to do with the
crime or with the Morellis, but that, after consideration, Madeiros had decided not to make any exceptions.

The driver's seat was not open long, however, for
Madeiros had dropped a clue which led promptly to
a more likely candidate. Under examination he had
dropped the word "Polish or Finland." Now when
Jimmie Weeks was being questioned by the detective
after Mr. Thompson's first visit, he stated that
Madeiros had spoken of the South Braintree crime

in the presence of "Steve Benkosky." [8] Mr. Thompson's second interview with Weeks concerning the detective's visit brought this response:

"Yes, they asked me if Madeiros had ever told the story he had told me in the presence of others. I am quite sure that I told them that Madeiros had told about different parts of the affair in the presence of Steve Benkosky at the Lime Rock Inn. Steve Benkosky, the last I knew of him, was living in Pawtucket, and the last I read of him was that he was shot in a hi-jack battle. I know he was wounded. I don't know now whether he is alive or dead."

It appeared that Benkosky was known as "Steve the Pole." Before our suspicions were aroused in regard to Steve, Mr. Thompson had questioned Madeiros on the Lime Rock Inn incident. When asked where Steve was, he answered without the slightest hesitation, "up in Canada." Following the Benkosky clue to Pawtucket and Providence—the cities adjoin each other— I learned that Benkosky was a young highwayman, not one of the Morelli gang, but apparently a member of another circle which included Madeiros, Weeks, Mingo and Pachecho. To Pachecho, Madeiros had also told of running with the Morelli mob in 1920 and doing "stick-up" jobs in their company. Benkosky was scarcely a year older than Madeiros, and in April, 1920, had been less than twenty years of age. This corresponded to the Madeiros statement as to the age

[8] Erroneously reported "Barrister" by the police stenographer.

of the driver and with the description given by witnesses who had the best opportunity to observe him. His light hair and complexion also satisfied the requirements.

The discovery that Benkosky was not a Morelli gangster, but a young desperado friend of Madeiros, went far toward explaining Madeiros' attitude if Steve were the driver. It cleared up Madeiros' earlier attempt to include the chauffeur as one of "four Italians" and his quick lie that Benkosky was "in Canada." It also tended to explain why Weeks never repeated any statement of Madeiros concerning the driver. Later when I asked Weeks informally what Benkosky had said at Lime Rock Inn at the time of the talk by Madeiros, he told me that Steve remarked, "Keep your trap shut."

Neither Weeks nor Madeiros, however, needed to fear that any statement of his would harm Benkosky. Calling at Steve's home in Pawtucket, I spoke to his heart-broken sister, who told me of an early-morning knock at the door only a few months before. In the gray light preceding dawn they had found the riddled body of Steve huddled on his own doorstep. Whatever else this young man may have been, it was apparent that he had been an idol in his own family and had shared with them his moments of prosperity. His young sister believed him innocent of all wrong-doing, despite court records, police and the press, an attitude which made it embarrassing for me to press for a

photograph of her brother. Later, however, I obtained
a rogues' gallery picture from the Providence police.
This picture, as will be seen, did not share the oblivion
accorded the likeness of Ray McDevitt.

Our hypothetical murder party now lacked but one
member—the bandit described by Madeiros as being
about thirty-five years old, and designated by him
as Bill. In his case the mental characteristics were
even more important than the physical, because he
was marked by extreme audacity and cruelty. His
bullets were found in the bodies of both Berardelli
and Parmenter and were fired almost in the presence
of a hundred horrified eyes. Unanimously nominated
for the post was Joe Morelli's close friend, Tony Mancini. He was generally conceded to be the "big job"
man of the gang, a New York product, quiet, determined, and dangerous. Investigation disclosed that
he was at liberty on April 15, 1920, and was thirty-
three years of age at the time. His dark coloring was
similar to that of Joe Morelli, and both answered in
this respect the description of eye-witnesses. The New
York police furnished us with a small photograph.

"Two short men," the District Attorney had said in
his opening to the jury, "perhaps five feet six or seven,
rather stocky . . . between 140 and 160 . . . of
apparent Italian lineage."

"Joseph Morelli," read the Providence police records, in late 1919, "Receiving Stolen Property, Height
5 feet 6 inches, weight 147."

"Antonio Mancini," echoed the records of the New York police in early 1921, "Crime Homicide, Height 5 feet 5 inches, weight 148."

# CHAPTER SIX

# "THE MAN I SAW"

WHICH OF the bandits had been mistaken by witnesses for Nicola Sacco? The record of the testimony seemed to answer "several of them." If one follows the story of the identifying witnesses it becomes obvious that these persons did not see the same man because no human being could have made such lightning changes of place and costume.

Sacco is first seen by Lola Andrews from 11.20 to 11.35 A.M. under an automobile in front of the lower factory of Rice and Hutchins. At that time he is wearing a dark suit. Five minutes later—or according to some of the testimony, at exactly the same time—he is standing with his back to Torrey's drugstore in South Braintree Square, dressed "respectably," according to the witness Tracey. At 12.27, the witness Heron saw him smoking a cigarette in the South Braintree depot, wearing dark "ordinary wearing apparel" and a soft black hat. The witness Pelser identified Sacco as the man shooting Berardelli and at that time Sacco had changed into dark green pants and a brown

85

army shirt. A few seconds later Miss Splaine sees him in a gray woolen shirt, wearing no hat or coat. According to the Government's theory, Sacco has now lost a cap, although he made his first appearance in South Braintree in a soft felt hat. As the automobile glides past Miss Splaine's vision for a few yards it passes Magazu's poolroom and by this time Sacco has resumed his dark suit, according to the witness Goodridge.

No evidence is more subject to error than the identification of unknown persons. Police records are full of the most extraordinary mistakes. The chances of error are further increased when the subjects identified belong to a group unfamiliar to the observer. "All coons look alike to me" expresses a psychological truth. In this case, however, the discovery that three brothers were involved in the crime, and that, in addition, Mancini, in general appearance, could have looked like Joe Morelli at a distance, explained a fertile basis for confusion. Mr. Richards had told us that the brothers were all the same type, short, dark muscular fellows, but we did not then appreciate the significance of the observation and never incorporated it in an affidavit. Nevertheless, the description of Mike and Frank by Sergeant Jacobs, and the descriptions of Joe by others, indicated a general similarity in build and coloration. We had no pictures of Frank and Mike. The likenesses of Pasquale and Joe showed marked family resemblances, but Pasquale was not

nominated by Madeiros for any post in South Braintree.

Nicola Sacco was twenty-nine years of age on the
date of his arrest in early May, 1920. The records
show that he was one inch shorter than Joe Morelli,
but exactly the same height as Mancini. On the other
hand, he was exactly the same weight as Morelli and
but one pound lighter than Mancini. The build of each
of them is listed as "medium." Sacco and Morelli
were darker than Mancini, all had dark hair, Sacco
and Mancini brown eyes and Morelli dark gray eyes.
To a stranger, seeing any of these three men at a
distance for a few seconds in great excitement, mistake in identity was easy. At the time and scene of
the crime witnesses who thought they saw Sacco
might well have seen either Joe Morelli or Mancini.

We felt, however, that the case of mistaken identity
turned around Morelli rather than Mancini. It has
already been mentioned that there were several Colt
thirty-two calibre automatics around the house of Joe
Morelli. At the trial, a single bullet fired through such
a pistol had been produced as having been extracted
from the body of Berardelli. When arrested, Sacco
had in his possession a thirty-two calibre Colt automatic.[1] It seemed reasonable, therefore, to suppose

[1] Sacco claimed that the weapon had been a protection to him in making
the nightly inspection of the factory, a duty which his employer, Mr.
Kelley, had entrusted to him. Mr. Kelley knew about the pistol and
had offered to assist Sacco in obtaining a license.

that Joe had enacted the rôle assigned to Sacco. At this time neither Mr. Thompson nor I doubted the genuineness of this bullet and it was not until a year later that we lost confidence in this exhibit as well as in an unmarked shell alleged to have been found at the scene. There was further good reason, however, for believing that Mancini was not the bandit charged with firing the single bullet from the Colt, but was the other bandit who apparently poured the shots into Parmenter. From all that was known about the two men, Mancini was more apt to be the cool and ruthless executioner. We were soon to receive startling confirmation of our tentative assumption that it was Joe Morelli who had been mistaken for Sacco.

No witness had claimed that Vanzetti was one of the bandits on the streets of South Braintree, nor was there any evidence that he had fired any of the bullets. Moreover, he was neither short nor stocky, and was marked by a long, heavy brown mustache whereas the described bandits were smooth shaven. One witness had testified that Vanzetti was the driver of the murder car, but so overwhelming was the testimony that the chauffeur was a pale, blond, young man that even the District Attorney practically repudiated the identification. There was no question, therefore, of Vanzetti being confused with either of the two criminals.

In the preceding chapter the mental and moral characteristics of members of the Morelli gang were considered. These men, we urged, were implicated as the murderers of Berardelli and Parmenter. It will be helpful to an understanding of the new evidence if I now present a brief sketch of the men whom the Commonwealth claimed committed this atrocious crime.

Nicola Sacco was born in the Province of Foggia, in southeastern Italy, near the shores of the Adriatic. His family were people of considerable substance, providing a mayor and other officials for the community, and Nick as a boy learned to love nature among the pleasant olive orchards and vineyards owned by his father. Thus he did not come from either the locality or the stock usually associated with Italian criminals in America. Prior to his arrest, he had never been accused of any crime. He was a highly skilled artisan, earning very high wages—frequently over seventy dollars per week—out of which he supported a family and accumulated a savings account of over fifteen hundred dollars. His employer had known him for many years and trusted him implicitly. Industrious, reliable, kindhearted [2] and fun-loving, "Nick" had all the qualities of a respectable citizen except one—he believed fanatically that government was merely a tool by which the "capitalists" oppressed the "working classes." Therefore he evaded the draft, sympathized with strikers, and followed the humble orator Vanzetti, whom he adored. His disbelief in

[2] Sacco gave to his employer the excess vegetables from his "war garden" to distribute among the poor of the town.

government classified him as an anarchist, but he was far from the lunatic, skulking bomb-thrower usually associated by the public with the word.

Whenever I visited Sacco he greeted me with a cheery smile and warm hand-clasp. Few men, after six or seven years of dreary prison idleness, could have maintained his spirit.[3] At first the shock of conviction and prison life had deranged his mind, and that of Vanzetti as well, but both men had recovered sanity. The record of Sacco's thoughts while in prison is contained in the published *Letters of Sacco and Vanzetti*,[4] which disclosed a nature remarkable for simplicity and great tenderness. He was always polite —even in heated argument. Convinced that his prosecution was a capitalist plot, he became extremely obstinate and would do nothing to help his defense— even declining to sign necessary papers. He was willing to shake hands with the Governor, for that was good manners, but not to discuss the case with him. When Mrs. Ehrmann remonstrated with him for not signing the appeal to the Governor and asked him to do it for love of his wife and children, Sacco burst out, "Excuse me! I no love Rosina if I not true first to myself!" Sacco's obstinacy and great sense of personal dignity made him such a very unsatisfactory prisoner, when compared to his more reasonable com-

[3] Until April, 1927, Sacco was technically "awaiting" sentence and therefore was not permitted to work.
[4] The Vanguard Press, 1930. The Viking Press, 1928.

panion, that gossip among the guards found Sacco
guilty but Vanzetti innocent. His obduracy during the
last year would occasionally evoke the Olympian
temper of Mr. Thompson, who would then discharge
himself as Sacco's counsel in a torrential wrath
while the object of it all stood resolute and amazed,
able to grasp only the general significance of the sacred and profane eloquence which deluged him.
Despite these occurrences, however, Mr. Thompson
continued to act as Sacco's counsel at the same retainer, which by this time had sunk to nothing.

Sacco's predominant qualities of steadfastness,
politeness and tenderness were all manifest in the
report of his conduct at the moment of his execution.
He walked firmly into the death-chamber and, at a
motion from the guard, took his seat in the electric
chair. As he did so, he shouted in Italian, "Long live
Anarchy!" He then paused, growing calmer, and said
in broken English, "Farewell, my wife, my child and
all my friends." Then, glancing around the room
which he seemed to see for the first time, he said to the
assembled witnesses, "Good-evening, gentlemen." And
as the hood was being slipped over his head, he mur-
mured in Italian, "Farewell, Mother."

Vanzetti was born in Piedmont, in Northern Italy,
and also came from a sturdy, self-sufficient race. In
the remarks made by him at the time of his sentence
he referred to the prosperous condition of his family,
who would have provided for him had he not chosen

to work. Like Sacco, he had never been accused of any offense prior to his arrest and he, too, had earned a law-abiding reputation among his Plymouth neighbors, including the police. After coming to America he had worked hard, read much, and preached the rights of the "oppressed." His keen mind and reasonable nature made him a more satisfactory client and a less troublesome prisoner than the dogged and doctrinaire friend who shared his fate. Nevertheless, he understood Sacco fully and often explained his friend sympathetically to Mr. Thompson and me. Occasionally he would reprove Sacco gently for his cocksureness, and he took a mischievous pleasure in beating his young disciple at games which they were permitted to play together during the few weeks when both were at the Dedham jail in the spring of 1927. Mr. Barret, one of the deputies at the jail, told me that he once overheard them in the yard debating as to which of them had the better singing voice. He watched, unobserved, and saw Vanzetti take a position against the wall and heard him sing in the "sweetest voice I ever heard," the popular song *Let Me Call You Sweetheart*.

Possessions to Vanzetti were merely things to give away. The first time he met me he rushed to the guard for permission to give me a carved penholder, and when he pressed my hand for the last time in the death-house at Charlestown, he asked me to keep some of his precious books as a remembrance after his death. Once when I handed him a few dollars sent to him by a sympathizer, he returned it immediately with the request that I buy various articles fashioned by fellow prisoners and distribute them among a list of friends.

He loved children especially and was beloved by them. At the trial for the Bridgewater attempt, we get a characteristic glimpse of Vanzetti as the witnesses tell of seeing him on Christmas Eve—the attempted robbery had occurred that morning—stuffing money into the stockings of his little Plymouth friends. Vanzetti's desire to give things, however, was merely the expression of a spirit deeply concerned with human beings. Once when I took a noted journalist to visit him, Vanzetti spent the entire time discussing the injustices of the Mooney case and never once mentioned his own predicament. He was then under sentence of death to be executed in a few months. In correcting a draft of his appeal to Governor Fuller, Vanzetti struck out the words "we are opposed . . . to communists and socialists" and substituted "opposed . . . to communism and socialism." He did not hate any people—only what they did and what they thought. Facing Judge Thayer on the morning of his sentence, he could not even then express himself vindictively against the man who had presided at both his trials, who, he believed, had caused his suffering and who had cursed him at country club and football field. "Maybe your Honor—I am sorry to say this because you are an old man, and I have an old father—but maybe you would be beside us in good justice at this time." His last words spoken slowly and calmly as he was being strapped into the electric chair disclosed the same serenity, the same kindliness, and the same precise expression of thought:

"I wish to thank you for everything you have done for me, Warden. I wish to tell you that I am innocent and that I have never committed any crime but sometimes some sin. I thank you for everything you have done for me. I am innocent of all crime, not only of this, but all. I am an innocent man. I wish to forgive some people for what they are now doing to me."

The rogue's gallery pictures of these two men were mingled with photographs of Joe, Pasquale, and Fred Morelli, Barone, Mancini, McDevitt, Benkosky and Madeiros in order to make up a portfolio which could fairly be submitted to witnesses.[5] It had not been easy to obtain most of these photographs. In Providence and New York we were compelled to use a letter which Mr. Ranney courteously furnished us, written on official stationery of the District Attorney's office. As a

[5] The "identifications" of Sacco and Vanzetti were obtained by displaying them alone to numerous witnesses instead of mingling them, in the accepted modern police method, with other men. They were even posed like the bandits during some of the inspections. To suggestible minds the inference must have been almost irresistible. In one instance only was there a "parade", but as this witness had a picture of Vanzetti in his possession before he made the inspection, there was no sense in the precaution.

member of the Boston Bar I anticipated no difficulty in seeing the head of the local bureau of identification. But when I formally applied for permission to the Superintendent of Police he curtly told me that he would not assist me in my effort to free "two murderers." I then appealed to the Commissioner of Police, who telephoned the Attorney-General of the Commonwealth for advice. This high officer of state apparently ruled in my favor, whereupon I was advised that the Boston Bureau had no record of the men named by me. This was not at all satisfactory, as I had desired to discuss the matter thoroughly with the head of the bureau, but I had to accept it.

However, obtaining the pictures was child's play compared with getting witnesses to look at them. For obvious reasons we preferred to have them examined by witnesses for the Commonwealth, since the defense witnesses were already discredited by the verdict. The case had stirred up so much feeling, however, and such wild unreasonable fears were rampant, that the task at first seemed impossible. On one occasion, a trained investigator for the Boston and Maine Railroad, showed some of the photographs to a woman witness and the next day the press screamed in the headlines that this lady had been visited by a "mysterious stranger" and that a "double guard" had been placed upon her home. The husband of another witness would not unlock the screen door when we called, using the well-worn formula of timidity—"We don't

want to become mixed up in the matter." In another
case, some man had stepped from behind a tree and
frightened the wife of a witness. It was difficult to
blame these poor people, as the press kept one's nerves
on the jump. Every explosion was blocked on the front
page into a "Sacco-Vanzetti Bombing," when, so far
as evidence was concerned, it might have been caused
by gas, home-brew, bootlegger's grudge, racketeering,
or what-not. In 1927 even practical jokes were reported to have appeared as "Sacco-Vanzetti Death
Threats."

But fear of radical activity was not the only apprehension felt by witnesses. One government witness at
the trial had refused to positively identify Sacco. He
had been an old employee of Slater and Morrill, but
was discharged after the trial and remained out of
work for a long time. To his mind there was only one
reason for the discharge. Another old and reliable
employee of Slater and Morrill refused to identify
either Sacco or Vanzetti for the prosecution and was
later called as a defense witness. After the trial he,
too, was dismissed and his position filled by a juryman. He had his own idea as to the reason and, need-
less to say, it was not that told him by the foreman.
At no stage of the investigation did we so feel the lack
of the compelling power of the State as in this simple
process of getting witnesses to look at pictures.

Our range of activity, however, was otherwise re-
stricted. Some witnesses had left the Commonwealth

and others could not be located. Other government witnesses were so discredited that it was a waste of time
to look them up.[6]

So far as the driver of the car was concerned, we
had the good fortune to discover the two witnesses best
qualified to describe him. They were young women in
the employ of Slater and Morrill who worked before
an open window not more than ten feet from the murder car as it stood prior to the shooting. They watched
the young chauffeur for at least half an hour. These
witnesses were not known to the defense before the
trial. They had been shown many pictures by the state
police and otherwise given much attention by the
Commonwealth, but were not called at the trial for
some unexplained reason.[7] Instead, the Commonwealth

[6] Three who identified Sacco were clearly of this description: One, a
crook with a lengthy record, who on recommendation of the District
Attorney, had been given probation for grand larceny shortly before
the trial and who had told numerous conflicting stories; another, an
hysterical woman of bad reputation, with a record for making false
claims against insurance companies, who also had given several different versions of the shooting, and the third, a young man who,
according to the District Attorney, "falsified to the defense . . . falsified to the Commonwealth."

[7] We argued before the Massachusetts Supreme Judicial Court that it
was the District Attorney's duty to put these young women on the
stand or reveal their names to the defense. The court at first held that
it was not improper for a prosecuting officer not to call a witness "in
whom he has no confidence *or* whose testimony contradicts what he is
trying to prove." This doctrine met our point but seemed to sanction
the suppression of evidence. It was later revised by substituting the
word "and" for the word "or." This revision was not subject to the
same criticism, but unfortunately did not decide the point which we

produced a witness who glimpsed the driver and a pistol muzzle for a few seconds, and claimed that Vanzetti was the man. This tended to carry the case against Vanzetti to the jury, even though the District Attorney himself conceded that the witness was obviously mistaken.

Our investigator called upon these two witnesses, Mrs. Kennedy and Mrs. Louise (Hays) Kelly, separately and showed them our photographs.. Each of them unhesitatingly selected the same picture as closely resembling the man she saw. Neither would state positively that the likeness was one of the driver of the car because of one circumstance—the face in the rogue's gallery picture was fuller than that of the young man before their window. Both admitted that the photograph looked more like the driver than any they had seen and they had inspected many for the State police. The subject of the photograph which claimed their attention was Steven Benkosky, or "Steve the Pole," as he appeared before the lens of the police camera on February 18, 1925. Possibly Steve had put on weight in the five years following the murder; perhaps these earnest young women were mistaken.

The judgment of these witnesses, however, was confirmed by one of the defense witnesses, Donato Di Bona. This man had testified to getting a look at the

had raised since there was never the slightest suggestion that the District Attorney had no confidence in these witnesses.

driver and the man who sat beside him as the car moved away after the robbery. He studied the different pictures for a week and finally selected for the driver—Steve Benkosky, and for the other man on the front seat—Antonio Mancini. These selections made us feel fairly sure of Steve the Pole, and encouraged, but did not convince us, as to Mancini.

The real surprise, however, came from the picture of Joe Morelli. We received some intimation of what was coming when the investigator and I hunted up a government witness in Brockton. At first he refused to talk to us, but upon my companion giving him a lodge password, he permitted an interview. At the trial he had declined to identify either Sacco or Vanzetti, although he had a good view of the bandits. Taking our collection he ran through them perfunctorily, recognizing without difficulty the photographs of Sacco and Vanzetti. Suddenly he stopped, picture in hand.

"I've seen this fellow before," he said, holding out Joe's photograph. On being informed whose likeness it was, this witness stated that he had thought the picture was one he had seen before, but had been mistaken. It struck us as a bit curious that the face had seemed familiar to him.

A short time thereafter, however, I showed the photographs to a group of Italian granite cutters at Quincy. They had been defense witnesses at the trial, and had made no identification. When I saw them they protested that they could not identify the men they saw after six years. A rather strange incident happened, however, when the first witness started running through the pictures. He began crying "Sacco! Sacco!" and the others crowded around him and took up the cry. I looked over his shoulder and saw that he was holding up the rogue's gallery likeness of Joe Morelli.

This occurrence impressed me considerably. Here were Italians who had watched their fellow countryman, Sacco, at the trial, yet they had mistaken the picture of another for that of Sacco. Perhaps there was a basis, other than general appearance, for some of the American witnesses to make a similar mistake. I took the pictures of Sacco and Morelli to the light and studied them. The comparison brought out amazing similarities. The heads of both were shaped alike; on both the hair was wavy and grew sparse around the temples; both had noses that tended to flatten at the tip; the ovals of the face were similar except that Sacco's jaw seemed squarer; the spacing of the features on both men was almost identical. There was, of course, no comparison between the expressions of the two faces, but this could not have been discernible at a short distance.

Mr. Lewis L. Wade, government witness at the trial, testified that Sacco resembled the man he saw, but that he had a doubt. He did not wish to see the investigator or me, or to give us an affidavit. When he was finally induced to look over the pictures he selected the photograph of Joe Morelli as "strikingly like the man whom I saw shooting Berardelli." He also stated that the picture resembled Sacco.

The investigator paid a visit to Mary (Splaine) Williams, star identification witness for the Commonwealth at the trial. He reported that she picked out Joe Morelli's picture, examined it closely, became a trifle excited and exclaimed, "This is a picture of the man who did the shooting! It's a picture of Sacco, isn't it?"

Mrs. Williams denied using the language related by the investigator. Her own version of what happened, however, was practically as significant.

"I said, Mr. Carter [she was referring incorrectly to the investigator], if you had seen Sacco's picture in the papers as often as it has been, and this one alongside of it, you would admit there was a resemblance, but from the picture you can't tell whether the man has the same complexion that Sacco has, neither can you tell whether he has the same large hand. . . . I told him that from the two pictures I wouldn't be willing to say that I was mistaken until I knew other characteristics about the man's looks. . . . I couldn't tell from the picture that this other man had the same distinctive features that Sacco has, referring to the complexion of the man and the large hand, that the picture did not show."

We need not worry with Mrs. Williams about the complexions of the two men. As for the "large hand, denoting strength," upon which she always insisted, we asked one of the leading haberdashers of Boston to measure Sacco for gloves. He reported, "I find Sacco has what men in the glove trade would call small hands." As for Joe Morelli, it is at least interesting to know that the Federal District Attorney asked him, during the trial in Providence, whether he had not boasted of the great strength of his hands, that he could hang to a freight car with one hand and open the door with the other.[8]

Not all of the witnesses, however, were confused by the resemblance of the men. A strong defense witness whom I sought all over Boston without success was Frank J. Burke. He had got an excellent view of one of the bandits and from the antics which this robber was performing in the automobile it must have been the same man seen by Splaine and Wade. Burke was a glass-blower by profession and had disappeared completely so far as we could trace him. In the early summer of 1926 I visited Norumbega Park with our children and my younger son dragged me to a glass-blowing exhibition. Suddenly recalling the business of the missing Burke, I asked the exhibitor whether he knew his fellow glass-blower. Apparently I had spoken to one of Burke's best friends and the next day a telegram found the missing witness in a Rhode Island town. When Burke saw the sheaf of photo-

[8] This question of the District Attorney was never incorporated into an affidavit because Joe denied that he had made the boast.

graphs he ran through them rapidly, indicating which was Sacco and which Vanzetti. Like the others, Burke stopped at the likeness of Joe Morelli and studied it for some time. Suddenly he slapped the face of the picture and exclaimed:

"That's the fellow! That's the fellow who snapped his pistol at me and yelled, 'Get out of the way, you son of a b——!' "

# CHAPTER SEVEN

## PRISON VOICES

FRANK SILVA, alias Paul Martini, received a visitor in the Federal prison at Atlanta during the year 1921. His caller was Fred H. Moore, who had represented Sacco at the trial for the Braintree murders. Mr. Moore was drawn to Atlanta by a rumor that Silva was one of the highwaymen who had attempted the Bridgewater hold-up for which Vanzetti had been previously convicted. Although he had never represented Vanzetti, Mr. Moore rightly divined that the conviction of Vanzetti at Plymouth for the Bridgewater attempt had blasted the way for the murder verdict at the Dedham courthouse. Once Vanzetti had been notoriously branded as a highwayman, the Dedham jury was naturally ready to believe the worst of the fish pedler and his shoemaker companion. And by a twist in the law of evidence due to Vanzetti's prior conviction, this jury was never permitted to hear testimony as to the excellent reputations of both defendants.

For some reason, nothing came of Mr. Moore's

interview with Martini. Years later, however, too late
to help the executed Sacco and Vanzetti, Martini's
tongue was loosened and he told in great detail the
story of the raid on the pay-truck of the L. Q. White
Shoe Company at Bridgewater, the day before Christmas, 1919. According to Martini, the attempted highway robbery was committed by himself and other
criminals. All of this matter, with its complete vindi-
cation of Vanzetti, was included in an article by
Silas Bent in the *Outlook and Independent* for October 31, 1928.

There was another prisoner at Atlanta, however,
who must have learned of Mr. Moore's visit with some
consternation. This person was Joe Morelli, serving a
twelve-year sentence from the Federal Court of Rhode
Island. At that time Moore had never heard of Morelli's name in connection with the South Braintree
murders. He was interested in Martini and a different
crime. Nevertheless, Morelli behaved in a strange
manner. Scarcely had the lawyer left Atlanta, when
Morelli, Martini and a prison pal named Luban, began to arrange an alibi for April 15, 1920, the date
of the Braintree crime. For this purpose they approached a fellow prisoner named Moller, who had a
typewriter in prison which he used in the interest of
Morelli, Martini and Luban, and arranged for all of
them to swear to the alibi. Moller later stated, "that
I was to testify that on the night particularly of April
fifteenth I was playing poker with Paul Martini and

Jake Luban and Joe Morelli and myself. That the game lasted the entire night. That prior to that time and after I had been living at the American Lodging House, Forty-sixth Street, which was then being run by the wife of Luban." Moller further stated these three men had been acquainted before they were in Atlanta, and also that, although the talk about the alibi seemed to be partly for the benefit of Luban and Martini, it was, in his opinion, really for the benefit of Joe Morelli, who did not wish Moller to suspect his connection with the South Braintree crime.

This statement by Moller was obtained as the result of a letter which he had written to the Boston Bar Association under date of November 1, 1923. Moller had recently been released from Atlanta only to land in jail in Washington, D. C. The letter was referred to Mr. Moore, who, in turn, sent a representative to interview Moller in the Washington prison. This investigator took pencil notes of the exact language used by the prison typist from Atlanta. The information probably meant little to Mr. Moore, who was then struggling with a mass of rumors, clues and expenses. Joe Morelli's action in 1921, however, took on a fresh and deeper meaning when, in 1926, the finger of circumstance pointed him out as the author of the South Braintree crime. Unfortunately, all trace of Moller was lost following his deportation in 1924 from Providence, where he was carrying on some activity on behalf of Joe Morelli.

By the summer of 1926 Joe Morelli had reached
the penitentiary at Leavenworth, Kansas, whither he
had migrated via several Federal penal institutions,
gathering along the way, as we have been told, com-
mendations from wardens and execrations from disillusioned fellow prisoners. Early in our investigation
an interview with Joe seemed desirable and I asked
Mr. Richards, the former U. S. Marshal, to accom-
pany me on the trip. As Mr. Richards knew all about
the gang and had been solicited in behalf of a parole
for Joe, we felt that his presence might have some
effect. It happened, therefore, that on June 1, 1926,
Mr. Richards and I got off the Santa Fé at Kansas
City, drove by automobile to the Federal penitentiary
at Leavenworth, and presented a letter of introduction
to the warden.[1]

As soon as we had made our mission known to the
warden, he showed considerable excitement, accusing
us of seeking to have Morelli "take the murder on his
shoulders." We assured him that such was not our
purpose, whereupon he exclaimed, "Morelli is a trusty
and if you get him all worked up he might make a
break!" Richards and I exchanged glances when we
heard this, because it indicated that Joe, as usual,
had succeeded in playing the game. We never fully
understood the rather strange conduct of the warden
during our visit. Later we learned that the administration of the prison was under investigation at the time

[1] Not the present warden.

by agents of the Department of Justice, and possibly this fact accounted for the warden's general attitude of nervousness and suspicion. At any rate, he finally made an appointment for us to see Joe later in the day, declaring that Morelli did not have to talk and that he would not be present.

When we returned at the hour set, Joe and the warden were in the waiting room and all of us marched together into the private office. Mr. Richards said, "Hello, Joe," and received a defiant grunt for a response. We sat down at the warden's table, Morelli alongside the warden, Mr. Richards and I facing them across the table. The warden then explained that the law required him to be present at the interview. Mr. Richards then introduced me to Joe, who acknowledged the presentation with a hostile glare that indicated some familiarity with the subject matter of our visit.

The early part of the interview consisted of immaterial preliminary statements by Mr. Richards and repeated denials by Morelli. Mr. Richards mentioned the letters written to him by Joe, who thereupon declared he had written no letters. Mr. Richards then referred to an acquaintance who had been to see him regarding Joe's application for a parole, but Joe denied knowledge of his own friend and claimed that he had sent no one to see Richards. He was then asked whether he knew Mancini. Joe's first answer was a denial, but after several repetitions of the name, he

said "Which Mancini? There are lots of Mancinis."
When Mr. Richards said he meant "Tony Mancini, the
one that got twenty years for killing a man," Morelli
commented, "I never heard of that."

It was heavy going for Mr. Richards, because every
time he started to say anything, Joe interjected a
denial. Finally Mr. Richards decided to plunge into
the Madeiros confession, but he had hardly referred
to "a Portuguese" when Morelli broke in, "I don't
know any Portuguese!" He then remained silent long
enough to learn that he and others were accused in
Massachusetts of committing the payroll robbery and
murders, whereupon he commented gravely, "I never
work with others; I always work alone." He denied
that he had ever heard of South Braintree or the Rice
and Hutchins or the Slater and Morrill factories.
When we reminded him that his conviction was on an
indictment containing counts for stealing shoes
shipped from these same factories, he stated that there
were fifteen counts, that it was six years ago and he
couldn't remember what was in them.

Up to this point Morelli's attitude had been one
of fear and defiance. When Mr. Richards finished his
narrative, Joe exclaimed that this was just another
attempt to put him away, like the "frame-up" for
which he was serving twelve years. Upon being accused of "framing" this notorious character, Mr.
Richards then explained to the warden how Morelli,
at the end of a long trial, had suddenly sprung a

charge that the Judge was not fair, and that the District Attorney, the Marshal, and the railroad police had shared in his criminal projects. He told of Morelli's retractions of these charges, and started to relate some of Joe's early criminal activities in Providence, when he was stopped by an unexpected burst of real or feigned emotion.

"You are trying to spoil my record with my warden, my good warden!" cried Joe over and over again in a voice that whined and wept, and in a manner that suggested persecuted martyrdom. The warden seemed impressed by this blatant by-play and reprimanded Mr. Richards for mentioning such subjects. "How would you like to have such things said to you?" he queried Mr. Richards, and then in a fatherly way told Morelli that he did not have to say anything unless he cared to. Joe then calmed down and declared he had nothing to say. We later learned why the outburst occurred when Mr. Richards began to discuss Joe's career.

A duty still remained for me to perform, however, and I proceeded to make my plea in behalf of Sacco and Vanzetti. I have faced judges and juries in whose eyes I could read a cold dissent, but never have I approached a more hopeless task than that of endeavoring to induce this case-hardened criminal to admit his knowledge of a double murder. I could appeal to him only on idealistic grounds to which Joe was not peculiarly sensitive. Afterward I had to smile at my

effort; I am sure that Joe himself had a good laugh
after we left. During my plea, however, he dropped
one remark even more significant, as indicating consciousness of guilt, than his many absurd denials.

At the mention of the words, "Sacco and Vanzetti,"
Morelli asked whether these were the men he read
about in the papers. He then exclaimed, "Sacco?
Sacco? *See Mancini about that!*"

The entire trip to Leavenworth was worth this admission, coming as it did after an earlier attempt to
deny knowledge of Mancini. At least Mr. Richards
and I thought that this slip was full of significance,
but, like most of the evidence which our investigation
unearthed, it came to be completely ignored.

Instead of being moved by my eloquence, Joe demanded that we prove the charges against him and
send him to the electric chair. As he stated that he
had nothing to say, the warden declared the interview
over. I handed my card to the warden in the vain hope
that a miracle might later open Morelli's mouth to
something besides denials, and Mr. Richards and I
left them seated together in the private office.

The explanation of Joe's emotional outburst came
three months after our return, when a long-distance
call suddenly revealed that the chief of the Morelli
gang had been paroled and was once more among his
friends in Providence. The return from Elba was not
without its significant splendor, however. After six
years in the penitentiary, Joe had enough money

awaiting him to purchase a new car, hire a chauffeur, and rent and equip a new "restaurant" in his home city. Since regaining his liberty, Joe has been accused of a number of criminal enterprises, but until recently has escaped unscathed. A short time ago, however, he had the bad judgment again to run afoul of the Federal law and now stands sentenced for some counterfeiting enterprise. His interest in this highly specialized promotion would seem to indicate that his capacity to learn new crimes has not abated, and that he did not waste the opportunity of furthering his education while at the Federal prisons.

Joe's parole was quite unexpected by us and was obtained, as I understand, without the knowledge of the Marshal, the District Attorney or the Judge who tried him. Only one of our acquaintances had foreknowledge of his impending release. When Mrs. Monterio, in the summer of 1926, visited Celestino Madeiros in the Dedham jail, they discussed the Morellis. Mrs. Monterio had read about some of them being interviewed in the Providence police station by the Norfolk District Attorney.

"You know," she said, "they have got the Morelli boys."

At that time, Madeiros was lying down, resting on his elbow, but when she said this, he raised himself suddenly and said, "Have they got them?" Mrs. Monterio nodded her assent, whereupon Madeiros made this correct statement and prophecy, "with the exception of Joe, who got twelve years and is still in prison, *but he has served six and will get his parole this year!*" I offer no explanation as to how this condemned and confined prisoner knew what was about to happen to a fellow criminal in Kansas, but merely record the surprising and meaningful fact.

Joe Morelli had recommended that we "see Mancini about that," and it seemed a good suggestion. Accordingly, a few weeks later, I presented myself at the state prison in Auburn, New York. Everything here was in contrast with the experience at Leavenworth. I filed my letter of introduction at a desk and immediately received a pass into the interior of the prison. Once inside, I was ushered into a large waiting room where several prisoners were receiving visitors. My guide told me to wait here for Mancini and disappeared. There was no semi-hysterical warden, no denouncing of my mission, no interference with the conference, but just a simple, orderly routine for handling visitors.

I awaited Mancini with eagerness but no real hope of securing anything of value. As a matter of fact, I returned from Auburn empty-handed, without a thing of evidentiary value to be included in an affidavit. There were no incriminating lies and suspicious concealments as in the Morelli interview. Everything that occurred was seemingly as consistent with innocence as with guilt. And yet, in a way, my conference with this daring and ruthless killer was remarkable. It disclosed a man of great self-possession and seeming frankness, apparently unconscious of any morals, but with a keen interest in his fellow men.

Mancini walked briskly into the room with the soft rubber-shod tread of the prisoner. He greeted me with a hand-shake and a smile, revealing an even row of white teeth. I could not help but notice, however, that his eyes seemed clouded by a slight film, so that when he looked at you he did not seem to see you but some faraway object. I brought him the greetings of a Providence lawyer who had acted for him on occasion. Mancini seemed pleased, observing that this lawyer had vainly attempted to obtain his parole after he had served three years of his sentence. "Must have been too soon," commented Mancini. I agreed.

"How is Bibba Barone?" was the first question, quite in contrast with Joe's denial of everything. I was able to state that the Bibba was, or was not, in jail—I cannot now recall which. Thereupon I told Mancini about the Madeiros confession and some of the evidence which we had discovered. He listened most intently, but displayed no emotion. I told him about my visit to Joe Morelli at Leavenworth, whereupon he interrupted with, "How is prison life agreeing with Joe?" I thought of Joe's earlier attempt to conceal his intimacy with Mancini. Then I recalled the significant slip when Sacco's name was mentioned.

"Joe told me to see you about this affair," I said slowly, watching him closely.

"He must be eating something," replied Mancini simply, looking me squarely in the face.

"Joe isn't the only one," I replied. "In Providence they said that he would plan the job, but wouldn't tackle it without you beside him to give him courage." At this point, Mancini gave his estimate of Joe Morelli, deliberately, his gaze turned toward the window and the scene beyond.

"Unless you know that a man has killed, you can't judge what he is capable of doing." There was a long pause. It struck me as singular that Mancini had not only characterized Morelli's murderous potentiality, but, by his attitude, had accepted the essential truth of the Madeiros story. He explained.

"Take me for instance. If I hadn't been caught, I would not be known as a murderer. At that, they gave me too stiff a sentence. The cops disappointed me, for I relieved them of a man who was worse than I am. The man I killed had killed others." Mancini paused, then added, "It was his life or mine."

Then, very quietly, almost gently, he condemned people who tell on others.

"I have first-hand knowledge of Joe's trial in Providence. Gyp and Joe got nothing by blaming each other. They'd have been better off, or just as well off, if they hadn't given each other up. But if you're going to tell, why not tell the whole truth? Why didn't Madeiros tell a whole-story instead of a half-story? He might as well come clean if he started. If Madeiros wanted to tell a half-truth, he might have named as his confederates men who had died and then let the State believe it or not."

He did not recall Steve Benkosky or Jimmie Weeks by name. Jimmie's picture, however, looked very familiar to him. I had no photograph of Steve to show him at the time. He picked up Fred Morelli's likeness.

"Freddie wouldn't be in it. Fred was a good kid. He tried to take all the blame in the Federal case." Here Mancini paused. I showed him pictures of Sacco and Vanzetti.

"They're not stick-up men. That's not a stick-up man [pointing to Vanzetti's picture]. Of course, you can't judge only by a man's appearance—you can't be always right on that. But the type of Sacco and Vanzetti—they're radicals, not stick-up men. They believe in sharing what they have." Then Mancini sprang a surprise lecture on the case.

"The State didn't treat them squarely. That gun expert—the fellow, what's his name, that testified to make the jury believe he thought the bullet went through Sacco's pistol when that wasn't really his opinion." [2]

[2] Mancini had reference to Captain Proctor's testimony that in his opinion the so-called "mortal" bullet was "consistent" with having passed through Sacco's pistol. After the conviction, he stated his opinion to be that although he believed the bullet had been fired by a Colt, there was no affirmative evidence whatever that the bullet had passed through Sacco's Colt. He further stated that the question put to him by the District Attorney was pre-arranged so that he could

"Captain Proctor?"

"Yes, that's it—Proctor. And the Department of Justice—they should have kept out of it."

"You seem to know a lot about the case."

"Yes, I do—know all about the case—but only from what I read in the newspapers. I read all the crime news that's published, it's my diversion. Then we entertain ourselves by trying to guess what gang did this or that job. You know, every crowd has certain peculiar methods and quite often we can spot them by their tactics. It's a good game."

He stated that he had read about the Madeiros confession in the newspapers, but "couldn't figure the name as Italian." I then showed him the Madeiros statement and the affidavits that referred to him. He read with great interest and when he came to the parts where his name appeared, his breathing became much more rapid, but his expression remained undisturbed. After this, his attitude toward the Madeiros evidence changed from one of tacit acceptance to one of active criticism.

"Perhaps Madeiros just wanted notoriety," he suggested. When I showed him for comparison the rogue's gallery pictures of Joe Morelli and Nicola Sacco, he failed to see any resemblance. "Look," he said, pointing, "Joe has a rounder chin; look at this; look at

---

give this answer. Captain Proctor later stated to several persons that he had a positive opinion that the bullet had not passed through Sacco's pistol.

that," and so on, indicating alleged differences between the two men.

Then I made my plea to Mancini as I had to Joe Morelli. I appealed to his idealistic side and felt only a little less of an ass than I had in Kansas. Finally I ended by assuring him that hundreds of thousands of people believed Sacco and Vanzetti innocent, and that if he were guilty and volunteered the truth, he would have their respect and gratitude. If, however, we had to prove his complicity against his denial, and succeeded, then he would not have a friend to plead for clemency in his behalf. Mancini listened gravely, and when I had finished, expressed his regret at not being able to help me.

"I'm sorry I can't do something in this case—I would if I could. But there isn't anything I know. I hope they won't electrocute Sacco and Vanzetti. Killing them won't bring the dead to life."

Mancini's last remark was typical of his practical outlook. Such matters as killing innocent people did not disturb him greatly. Killing was deplorable only when it was useless. I also noticed that if he were guilty of the South Braintree murders, his lies had been sharply limited to essential matters. As he shook hands with me and wished me luck on the case, I felt that he could never be made to talk against his will, but that if he started, he would not tell a half-story. However, I had tried to make Mancini talk, but had failed. We had begun with the hypothesis that Man-

cini was the member of the Morelli gang most likely
to have shot down the paymaster and guard before a
hundred witnesses. We found that he was available
for the crime and that his appearance fitted the
descriptions of one of the street bandits. And Joe
Morelli, off his guard, had advised us to "see Mancini about that." Yet Mancini himself, although showing intimate knowledge of the trial of Sacco and
Vanzetti and a tacit acceptance of the Madeiros story
—until the evidence involved him—had said nothing
really incriminating. Somewhere, however, this criminal might have left a tell-tale fact more eloquent than
his own guarded speech.

The next day found me in New York City at the office of an old friend, Henry Epstein, a young lawyer,
now assistant attorney general of New York. I asked
Mr. Epstein to look up the crime for which Mancini
had been sentenced, with special reference to the type
of weapon used by him. I rather expected to find that
the weapon had not been discovered, or that the record
of its character had not been preserved. If Mr. Epstein
should be successful, however, I felt that no person
could really believe that mere coincidence, starting
with a slip of paper in the Dedham jail, could reach
back five years to Mulberry Street, New York, and
kill Mancini's victim with the same peculiar weapon
which ten months before had slain Parmenter and
Berardelli in South Braintree.

It now becomes necessary to refer to some of the

expert testimony given in the Sacco-Vanzetti case. There were produced at the trial six bullets claimed to have been extracted from the bodies of the murdered men and four exploded shells alleged to have been found at the scene of the crime. Only one bullet and one shell, however, was claimed to have been fired by Sacco and none by Vanzetti. No theory was advanced as to who fired the other bullets and shells. Nevertheless, the evidence as to these exhibits is most interesting. State expert Captain Proctor thought that the three shells had been fired by a single weapon, as had the five bullets. It was his opinion that the bullets had been fired through a Savage automatic, but on cross-examination, admitted he had never even heard of a Steyr pistol, one of the best known foreign automatics. He gave no opinion as to the type of weapon used to fire the shells. State expert Captain Van Amburgh thought the bullets "consistent" with having been fired through a Savage, but it was later learned that the technical meaning of consistent was simply "might have." He believed they were all fired from the same weapon. Captain Van Amburgh gave no opinion as to what weapon had fired the shells. On cross-examination he admitted his unfamiliarity with "foreign guns." Apparently, in 1921, foreign pistols with metric measurements were rather uncommon. Defense expert Burns, ballistic engineer for the United States Cartridge Company, however, was positive that the five bullets had been fired through a foreign auto-

matic of 7.65 millimeter calibre and designated the
"Steyr" make. Such a weapon will take thirty-two
calibre cartridges. He added that the bullets might
have been fired through a Savage, Steyr, or Walther,
made in Germany. Defense expert Fitzgerald did not
testify as to these bullets and shells. At the trial,
therefore, it appeared that the State experts believed
the bullets to have been fired through a Savage, but
disclosed unfamiliarity with foreign makes. Mr.
Burns, with knowledge of both foreign and domestic
pistols, unhesitatingly selected the foreign 7.65 millimeter. After the trial, defense expert Hamilton studied
the exhibits with the aid of powerful microscopic in-
struments and greatly enlarged photographs. He came
to the conclusion that the bullets had not been fired
through a Savage, and also that their markings were
completely matched by no American weapon, although Harrington and Richardson automatic corresponded in some particulars. Then Mr. Hamilton
turned his attention to the shells, apparently the first
expert to make deductions as to the type of weapon
from the shells, since the others had considered the
bullets only. Mr. Hamilton easily eliminated the
Savage as a possibility by pointing out that the photographs "reveal upon the side of the shell an ejector
or claw mark utterly unknown to a shell ejected from
a Savage pistol and impossible to be made by the
Savage mechanism." He then examined other American possibilities and concluded:

"From all of the above the affiant gives it as his unqualified expert opinion, with no reservations, that Fraher shells F1, F2, and F3, appearing on page one of the album and the same shells appearing again on page thirteen of the album, were not fired from any American-made automatic pistol, but were of necessity fired from some automatic pistol of foreign manufacture."

Although State experts filed many affidavits contesting other findings of Mr. Hamilton concerning the so-called "mortal bullet" and shell, none controverted his conclusions as to these other exhibits that no American weapon completely matched the bullet markings and that the shells had been fired through a foreign automatic. Indeed, as to the shells, the evidence, when pointed out, was quite obvious and conclusive. And there the matter rested until July, 1926, when I received the report of Mr. Epstein's investigation.

The story of how Mancini killed Alberto Alterio is told at the beginning of this history. The report as to the weapon read:

"The automatic pistol with which the murder was committed to which Mancini pleaded guilty and which was taken by Detective Dugan who made the arrest was a 'Star Automatic Pistol', of the calibre 7.65; the pistol No. 70480. There were found on the scene of the murder two discharged cartridges from said pistol and in the magazine seven undischarged cartridges.

This pistol it is reported by Mr. Foster of the Colt Arms Co. is found in two calibres, the smaller calibre corresponding to the twenty-five calibre automatics and the kind with which the murder was committed, namely, 7.65, corresponds to the thirty-two calibre automatics. This pistol is not manufactured in America and the only known agent is reported to be Adolf Frank, Hamburg, Germany."

The report also indicated that Mancini had carried the pistol in Providence before the time of the murder.

It is easy to picture our excitement on receiving this dramatic news. I immediately telephoned Mr. Epstein and asked him to offer a reward for the production of Mancini's pistol or bullets or cartridges. These items, however, had disappeared completely. Time had done its work, leaving only the record in the office of the District Attorney to speak in the face of Mancini's silence. We attempted to paint the lily by suggesting "Star" in the file was a mistake for "Steyr." Such an error was at least possible. State expert Van Amburg filed an affidavit alleging that a "Star" automatic was not a "Steyr," that neither was of American manufacture, but that both accommodated American-made cartridges as well as those of foreign manufacture. It did not matter much, however, since we had landed Mancini with a foreign automatic, 7.65 calibre. For even Captain Van Amburg no longer denied the basic fact that there was present in South Braintree, at 3 P.M. on April 15th, 1920, a weapon of this peculiar description, spitting its message of death and dropping shells marked by the tell-tale foreign ejector-claw.

CHAPTER EIGHT

# "ANSWER, BUT NOT

# INVESTIGATE"

WE HAVE been criticized for failure to investigate this matter jointly. That is the explanation. We believe we have found the truth, and in our judicial capacity—there is some to a District Attorney—having found the truth, nothing else can matter. And that is our honest conviction. And if that is so, it is a case not for investigation and we justify our position by that alone. We will answer, but not investigate, because we know or believe that the truth has been found."

In these words did the young Assistant District Attorney explain to the Court why his department had declined to accept Mr. Thompson's early suggestion for a joint investigation of the Madeiros confession. It is to be observed that the explanation went beyond its immediate object and offered a reason why no investigation whatsoever had been made, and such in substance was the fact. Except as will be described, the great power of the Commonwealth of Massachusetts remained passive and inert while we scurried around, inexpertly, to secure evidence from unwilling and often fear-stricken witnesses. The statement was certainly frank enough, as it was a clear notice to the world that nothing would be permitted to disturb the belief in the guilt of Sacco and Vanzetti. In the exercise of its "judicial" capacity, the District Attorney's office of Norfolk County had decided not to investigate any facts conflicting with that belief.

In stating this position, Mr. Ranney, the Assistant District Attorney, was voicing the official attitude of his department, not necessarily his own view. He had come into office after the case had been tried and was in no way responsible for it. The task assigned to him could not have been an agreeable one. If he carried out what I believe to have been a clearly wrong official policy, he nevertheless did it honorably and our relations were marked by straightforwardness and lack of suspicion. If we appeared to him to be enlisted in a bad cause, I hope that he regarded us as fair fighters. Mr. Ranney furnished us the letters that unlocked the rogues' galleries in Providence and New York, and, I believe, used his influence to stop State detectives from bullying our witnesses.

As answer, but not as investigation, apparently, the Commonwealth obtained and filed a few affidavits. Substantially all of these affidavits were intended to show either that Madeiros was not living in Providence on April 15, 1920, as he said he was, that the Morellis denied being guilty of the crime, and that

for one reason or another—unconnected with the corroborative evidence which we had obtained—Madeiros was unworthy of belief. It must not be supposed,
however, that the Commonwealth did not carefully
check up the progress of our investigation. There
were scattering affidavits on various matters, some of
which became immaterial and some designed to meet
detailed claims on our part. Among the latter were
Captain Van Amburgh's affidavit that the "Star" and
"Steyr" were different foreign automatics; Mary
Splaine Williams' denial of certain expressions attributed to her by our investigator, but admitting the
talk about the resemblance between the Sacco and Joe
Morelli pictures; a denial by the railroad detective
Karnes that Joe Morelli had taken him to South Braintree and shown him where shipments were spotted,
coupled with the agreement, however, by Mr. Ranney,
that Joe had taken Karnes to other Massachusetts
towns for this purpose. Beyond this, not a single
original fact uncovered by the investigation was controverted by the Commonwealth.

Mr. Thompson's plan for a joint investigation by
the State and himself was made, as he put it, to avoid
a "vulgar contest of affidavits." The wisdom of his
suggestion was apparent in the very first issue raised,
namely, whether or not Madeiros was in Providence
on April 15, 1920. Such a "vulgar contest" immediately resulted, but fortunately proved the last of
any considerable importance. I give the contest at

some length because it illustrates the folly of trying to settle a disputed point by such a method.

At the courthouse during the trial of Madeiros in May, 1926, Mr. Thompson, in the presence of Mr. Ranney, had asked certain questions of Madeiros' sister concerning her brother's whereabouts at the time in question. Her answers were not taken down, as they would have been in a joint investigation, and later Mr. Thompson and Mr. Ranney differed in their recollection of what she said. Both remembered that the sister had stated that she had lived in Providence, was unable to fix the exact year, and that Celestino had lived in a room adjoining hers for some of the time. Mr. Thompson recollected that she fixed the date of his leaving Providence as being one or two days before his arrest in New Bedford (his first arrest was May 1, 1920; his second May 25, 1920). Mr. Ranney did not recollect that she mentioned her brother's arrest and emphasized her almost complete lack of certain memory. He then filed an affidavit by Captain McKay, of the New Bedford police, to the effect that the Captain saw Madeiros in New Bedford in April, 1920, "practically every day."

When I saw Captain McKay he readily stated that he did not mean literally "every day," as it was perfectly possible that Madeiros might have been absent as long as a week without his knowing it and also that it was easy for a man to get from Providence to New Bedford and back again. As Madeiros was an officer

in the American Rescue League (its purpose unexplained), with both Providence and New Bedford in
his circuit, this was exactly what Madeiros was doing.
The Commonwealth then produced an affidavit from
Mrs. Matthews, Madeiros' sister, to the effect that she
went to Providence in January, 1920, was joined by
Madeiros "two or three weeks after" and he stayed
there "for about a month." State Detective Fleming
then made an affidavit relating to an interview he
claimed to have had with Mrs. Matthews on December
6, 1925. Although this was months before Mr. Thompson and Mr. Ranney had attempted to stir Mrs. Matthews' hazy recollection with such limited results, Mr.
Fleming had, apparently, anticipated them with complete and precise success. "She stated to me that in
April, 1920, she was living in a lodging house in
Providence . . . that her brother, Celestino Madeiros,
came to live with her at this house about four months
before his arrest on May 1, 1920, and stayed with her
less than two months. She stated that she was positive
that he was not living with her in Providence during
the month of April, 1920."

Prior to the filing of this affidavit, I had called upon
Mrs. Matthews accompanied by an official court reporter and a friendly member of the New Bedford
police. Mrs. Matthews apparently resented our presence and refused to give an affidavit. Nevertheless, on
being questioned, she stated before the three of us
that Celestino had had a room next to hers in Provi-

dence for about a month until he was arrested in New Bedford. This was almost precisely her previous statement in May as Mr. Thompson had recollected it. Under the plan for a joint investigation, Mr. Ranney and Mr. Thompson would have questioned Mrs. Matthews thoroughly in the presence of each other and before an official stenographer, thus saving an absurd waste of time and an unpleasant clash of recollections between lawyers.

Fortunately Mr. Thompson was not satisfied to rest the point on these variations of Mrs. Matthews. He commissioned Thomas O'Connor, a State House reporter interested in the case, to investigate the possibilities in Providence. Armed with photographs and the unusual circumstance of two young Portuguese in the uniforms of some kind of a relief organization, Mr. O'Connor patiently combed all of the possibilities and finally settled, beyond any serious question, the presence of Madeiros in Providence in April, 1920. He traced to Woonsocket the former owner of the lodging house where Madeiros and his sister had lived. Rubin Galkin had acquired the property about March 1, 1920, and clearly recollected Madeiros, his sister, and their superior officer "among others." He described them, their uniforms and their business perfectly, and stated that the younger man—Madeiros —roomed at his place for approximately three months in the spring of 1920. O'Connor also located a former resident of the lodging house, Patrick J. McGovern, who remembered the "army," as he called it, distinctly, and the individual members of it. He selected the picture of Madeiros out of seven handed to him by Mr. O'Connor. Mr. McGovern fixes their residence in April by the fact that he finished jury service on April 1, 1920.

"About two weeks after I had finished my jury service, somewhere between ten and eleven o'clock one night, as I was coming in to go to my room, as I passed the room of the younger man and the woman with the reddish hair, I noticed that they were having some trouble with the lock on the door. I paid no attention to it, but continued upstairs to my room. Soon after I had entered my room, and while I was taking off some of my clothes, there was a knock at the door and the younger man who stood at the door asked me if I had a key which would fit the door of his room. I told him that I had not; that I had no key to fit any door only the door of my own room; that I would let him take my key and he could try it and see if he could do anything with it. He took the key and went downstairs. After a few minutes, when he did not return, I went downstairs to his room to get back the key and I found the younger man and the woman with the reddish hair in the room and they were working at the lock on the door. The man said somebody had been tampering with the lock. I told him that I had roomed there for quite a while and had never missed anything out of my room. He told me he could not do anything with the key, so I tried the lock myself, to see if I could do anything with it, but I could not get the lug back into the lock so that the door could be closed. I told him I could not do anything with it and they said they would put a chair or something against the door until morning. I took back my key and went upstairs to my room and went to bed."

What had happened about the middle of April to suggest to Madeiros the advisability of locking his door?

Mr. O'Connor's thoroughness also discovered Mrs. Nellie Gannon of Providence, who with her husband had roomed in the same lodging house. She had no difficulty in recollecting the party and also selected Madeiros' picture from the group. Mrs. Gannon and her husband had frequently complained of the noise made by these young people during late hours of the night. She finally moved in the early part of May so as to escape the annoyance. In this manner Mr. O'Connor's research settled the issue and ended the "contest of affidavits."

The attempt to eliminate the Morellis from the picture provided the only comic relief to a terribly tragic reality. Only the music of Sir Arthur was missing to complete a perfect Gilbert and Sullivan topsy-turvy operetta. It is to be regretted, however, that the Commonwealth of Massachusetts sponsored the production.

In true Gilbertian style, the play opens with a mistake. Through a typographical error on the part of a stenographer at the Providence County jail— "May" for "March"—the Norfolk District Attorney's office is mistakenly assured that Joseph Morelli was in jail during April, 1920. By the time the warden discovered the error and corrected it, the play was half over. The District Attorney and his assistant, Mr. Ranney, interviewed Frank, Pasquale and Fred Morelli. These gentlemen are careful to include their attorney, a Mr. Kiernan of Providence, in the conference. They are not unwilling, however, to confirm a typographical error and assure the Massachusetts officials that "they believe Joe Morelli was in the Providence County jail during the month of April, 1920." This is solemnly recorded. Looking at a picture of Madeiros, each states that "he had never seen any person who resembled in any way the person pictured in that photograph." Although much of the stuff which they had stolen was shipped from the South Braintree factories and, therefore, spotted for them in that town, they each assure the officials "that they did not know where South Braintree, Massachusetts, was situated and that they had never at any time gone to said South Braintree." "They each further said that they had nothing whatsoever to do with the shooting of Parmenter and Berardelli or the robbery of the payroll of the Slater-Morrill factory on April 15, 1920." All of this is solemnly recorded.

Fred Morelli stated that he was in jail in April, 1920, which was true enough; he was the one Morelli in jail during the period. Frank, however, said he was in Providence during the entire month of April, 1920. But Sergeant Jacobs had seen him in New Bedford, acting somewhat suspiciously; his own lawyer at the time, Mr. Geary, knew that he had been in New Bedford; and Frank himself, testifying at his trial in 1920, stated that he had been in New Bedford but traveled about a good deal. They knew no person by the name of James F. Weeks, nor had they ever been to that wicked resort, the Blue Bird Inn, though they admitted having heard of it. The interview with these gangsters terminates on a note of high whimsicality.

"Dudley P. Ranney asked each one of the three persons whether he would sign and swear to a statement setting forth the said facts, but each of the said persons refused to do so, saying that he feared for his personal safety." There has been no scene like it since the *Pirates of Penzance* informed the police that they were orphans and noblemen gone wrong.

The next scene is at Leavenworth where a State detective interviews the gang chieftain. Joe tells this officer that he is an "expressman." At his trial, just prior to sentence, Joe had testified that he was in the piano business, the fruit and produce business, hens and chickens, and the restaurant business. The new occupation was probably one of Joe's little jokes, as he had expressed many thousands of dollars' worth

of stolen merchandise. Of course, Joe never knew
Madeiros and could not identify his photograph.
Asked the classical legal question, "Can you tell me
where you were April 15, 1920?" Joe does not hesi-
tate, although it was more than six years before: "I
went from my home to my lawyer's office, then to
Jones' restaurant, hang around and then drive home."
But what had become of the little alibi poker game
on that date, in New York, between Morelli, Luban,
Martini, and Moller? Joe then gives his version of the
visit which Mr. Richards and I had paid him and his
warden. Although he adds a few false dramatic
touches, such as my being introduced to him under
an assumed name, and our demanding that he "sign
a confession," the story is not unrecognizable.

One of the other Morellis now recovers from his
fear for his personal safety and furnishes the Commonwealth, through his lawyer, with an affidavit. The
affiant is Pasquale, who is not himself implicated in
the South Braintree crime.

"From the month of June, 1919, when I was honorably discharged from the United States Army," says
Patsy, not neglecting the patriotic note, "until the
month of May, 1920, I saw my brother Joseph Morelli, now confined at the United States penitentiary
in Leavenworth, Kansas, every night and every morning and almost hourly during every day between above
said dates." Terrible, if true! However, Patsy forgot that only a few weeks before he had informed the

District Attorneys that Joe was in the county jail during April, 1920. He also forgot that Joe had testified at his trial in May, 1920, of trips without his brothers, and of course did not know of the boastful growl to Mr. Richards and me at Leavenworth, "I always work alone."

The final affidavit of this series was by Joe's "housekeeper," an unfortunate woman with a long record for street-walking and kindred offenses, but a willingness to lie for Joe's benefit proven at his trial in May, 1920. This affidavit was also procured through Mr. Kiernan and gravely filed by the District Attorney. This lady pays a touching tribute to Joe's regular hours. "I further depose and say that the said Joseph Morelli was home every night during said month of April before twelve o'clock and that he did not leave the house on any night during said April until ten o'clock the following morning." At the trial in 1920, Joe had agreed with the District Attorney that after his arrest he had stayed out all night until "sometimes five or seven" o'clock, the only point of difference being that the prosecutor said he was stealing and Joe insisted that he was merely gambling. But Joe's "housekeeper" knew exactly when he came home and what time he left "from the year 1918 until he was sent to jail in May, 1920," adding to her affidavit this final touch: "I further depose and say that I was in a position to know—"

Mr. Thompson and I used this material filed by the

State to show conclusively the falsehoods and contradictions of the Morellis which had begun as early as
April 24, 1920, in Joe Fiore's restaurant when Frank
had lied to Sergeant Jacobs. Apparently, however, the
lies of criminals meant nothing as indicating consciousness of guilt; whereas the falsehoods of frightened radicals, arrested three days after a colleague
had been killed,[1] while in Federal custody, are almost
conclusive evidence of complicity in a payroll robbery and murder.

The last group of affidavits filed by the State were
intended to affect the credibility of Madeiros. Several
of these statements merely established the fact that
after learning of Madeiros' confession, Mr. Thompson
interviewed him in the open and semi-public rotunda
of the jail with Sacco present. It was Mr. Thompson
who sent for Sacco in the hope that the presence of
the man who had suffered for Madeiros' crime might
influence him to talk more freely. It was not denied
that Sacco's only contribution to the interview was to
implore Madeiros to tell the truth, "for Jesus' sake"
as Madeiros recalled, "for Christ's sake" as Mr.
Thompson remembered. Mr. Thompson immediately
sent his typewritten memorandum of the interview to
Mr. Ranney and no protest whatever was then made.

[1] On the morning of May 3, 1920, the body of Salsedo, a fellow anarchist, had been found crushed on the pavement outside the building
in Park Row where he had been "detained" by Department of Justice
agents.

As will be seen in the next chapter, the story told by Madeiros differed so drastically from the accepted version at the trial that it could scarcely be argued that Madeiros learned anything from Mr. Thompson or Sacco. For this reason, perhaps, no argument of any kind was ever based on these affidavits and they disappeared from view.

There was also an affidavit from Madeiros' sister, Mrs. Matthews, to the effect that he said to his mother and' sister when they visited him, "You think I am tough because I am in this case—well, there is a fellow in here over five years who killed two men in a job." Madeiros denied making the remark. The date of the visit was not fixed except that it was in the fall of 1925—and might have been before or after his written confession which was first made on November 16, 1925. The inference intended by the affidavit is that Madeiros believed that Sacco was guilty. Even if Madeiros had made the statement, however, it would not warrant such an inference since it might have represented merely his idea of comforting his old mother and nothing else. It seems unlikely, however, that he had made any such remark since at the same interview, apparently, his sister sought to have him retract the confession he had made. This was the same sister whose varying statements about Madeiros in Providence had led to such confusion of affidavits.

There was an affidavit from the jail official who had received and held up Madeiros' earlier written con-

fession of November 16, 1925, to the effect that immediately prior to writing this confession Madeiros had
sent for and received a financial report of the Sacco-
Vanzetti Defense Committee. This pamphlet showed
the expenditure of nearly three hundred thousand dollars but only a debit balance by July 31, 1925. Madeiros admitted that he had seen the report, but stated
it was brought to him at least a week after his written
confession. Madeiros was no paragon of veracity, but
what are we to say of the attitude of a jail official
who receives a confession exonerating two men convicted of murder, and does nothing to convey this vital
news to counsel for the men until more than six
months later and then files a hostile affidavit intended
to discredit the confession which he kept secret? Such
conduct hardly inspires confidence. Apparently, the
intention in filing this affidavit was to suggest a corrupt motive for the Madeiros confession. Mr. Ranney
made no such argument, however, and beyond char-
acterizing Madeiros as a psychopathic personality, he
assigned no motive for Madeiros' acts. It remained for
Judge Webster Thayer to build an elaborate argument for corruption out of this financial report of a
thoroughly insolvent organization, forgetting that, according to the evidence, and now corroborated by
another jail official through the fairness of Mr. Ranney, Madeiros had already told Sacco that he had
been in on the South Braintree job. Sacco, with one
experience of a spy in the next cell, had ignored these

attempts but had reported at least one such incident to the night officer who later confirmed his story.

Finally[2] there were affidavits from two alienists who examined Madeiros in April, 1926, prior to his second trial. Although their mission was to determine his sanity, they proceeded to cross-examine Madeiros concerning his confession to participation in the South Braintree crime. These physicians annexed some stenographic notes of the interview which indicate that Madeiros did not remember the year of the murders and also that he claimed that he did not know Sacco and Vanzetti were accused of the crime until he came to the Dedham jail. The lapse of memory was simply in line with Madeiros' inability to recollect any dates, as will be later seen. The other statement, if recorded properly, was undoubtedly a falsehood, as Madeiros had discussed the Sacco and Vanzetti case with both Weeks and Monterio. To Mr. Ranney on cross-examination Madeiros stated that these doctors had come to find out whether he was insane, that he couldn't see what right they had to question him, and that he told them the first things that came into his mind, whether true or not. Nevertheless, it is significant that when these doctors, unknown to counsel for Sacco and Vanzetti, cross-examined Madeiros apparently to shake

[2] To these should be added the deposition of Madeiros himself from which the District Attorney drew inferences unfavorable to our contentions. The statements relied upon by him will be considered in the next chapter.

his confession, he told them substantially the same
story he had related to Mr. Thompson. Not once did
he waiver.

"Q. Why did you want to make a statement of that
kind?

A. I rather not talk about.

Q. You must have had some purpose one way or
the other for giving out that information?

A. Maybe it is true."

Q. Would you want to go further and say maybe
or that it *is* true?

A. Yes.

Q. Is it true?

"A. Yes."

It was the same answer Madeiros was to give to
all inquirers, even to the Governor in a hurried col-
loquy at the State Prison shortly before the execution.
Always there was the same unbelief, the same effort
to get him to admit that he had lied. It was even reported that a prison chaplain had sought to induce
him to retract and that for this reason Madeiros
spurned the consolation of religion. At any rate, when
his last hour struck, Madeiros marched to the chair
unshaken and unshriven, followed immediately by
Sacco and Vanzetti. History had written that the execution of a thief was necessary to a perfect Calvary.

# CHAPTER NINE

## "MY DEAR WATSON"

MY DEAR Watson," a suppositious Sherlock Holmes might have observed upon glancing at the report of our investigation, "all of this evidence concerning the Morellis is very interesting and convincing, but so far as I am concerned, quite superfluous."

Were I the admiring Watson, this remark would have indicated to me that the great detective was in one of his rare talkative moods. Indeed, for the purpose of this chapter, I shall become the helpful Watson, letting the imaginary Holmes develop his thought in his own characteristic way. Now, as Dr. Watson, I push back my chair, light a cigarette and wait expectantly. Presently Holmes resumes.

"Quite superfluous for you to scurry around to Providence, New Bedford, New York, Worcester, Auburn, Leavenworth and those other places. Necessary, no doubt, for your case, but not needed by one accustomed to the inductive method of reasoning."

"You mean," I began—

"Exactly," said Holmes. "Even without the cor-

142

roborative evidence which you gathered, it was quite obvious that this fellow Madeiros possessed intimate knowledge of the murders at South Braintree. This could have been easily ascertained by a reasoned consideration of his story, his reported statements to others, and facts readily available."

"From the same evidence the Assistant District Attorney argued that Madeiros was a liar," I suggested, knowing that opposition always acted as a stimulant upon him.

"My dear Watson," replied Holmes, "Mr. Ranney, and, I might also add, Judge Thayer, were lawyers who measured everything by what they thought was the 'record.' Now the 'record' of a criminal trial is not the crime itself—it is merely what various witnesses think they observed and remember. Their accounts, and especially the emphasis on various incidents, will vary according to their temperaments, their opportunities to observe, their openness to suggestion and their memories.

"For example, one would hardly expect a criminal, for whom the whole day was one of preparation and excitement, to be impressed by the same things as factory workers who merely heard some shots, rushed to a window and saw an escaping automobile." Here Holmes chuckled.

"Even these witnesses did not agree among themselves. They assigned different colors to the car, described its condition variously, and gave the bandits so many rapid changes of costume that only a band of magicians could have qualified for the feat. But to return to Madeiros: In order to decide whether he has real knowledge, one must attempt to put oneself in Madeiros' place, with his mind and his eyes.

"Take one slight, but highly interesting example. What do you regard as the most significant statement made by his friend, Jimmie Weeks, who planned the Wrentham job with Madeiros?"

I thought a moment: "Well, I was impressed by the fact that they stole a Buick and a Hudson car for the Wrentham affair and that a Buick and probably a Hudson had been stolen for the South Braintree robbery."

"Madeiros certainly seemed to be patterning his project on the earlier crime," agreed Holmes. "In both cases the glass in the rear of the escape car had been removed and a weapon held in readiness to blow out tires of pursuing cars. However, similarity of technique is helpful, but by no means conclusive. You are warm, Watson, but no more."

I waited, somewhat chagrined, for Holmes to proceed.

"Don't you recall the little explanation given by Weeks as to why they stole a Hudson for the Wrentham job after they had already helped themselves to a Buick?"

"That Madeiros wanted a Hudson car to get away

with, as he had had enough of the Buick in the South Braintree job?"

"Exactly. Suppose you were one of the bandits, trying to get away from the scene of a robbery and possible murder. Would you be impressed if the motor didn't act properly?"

"Impressed? It would be the greatest anxiety in the escape."

"Then we agree. But would the flock of witnesses converging almost instantaneously upon a scene of murder and robbery be likely to note the fact that the escaping motor was missing a beat?"

"Hardly," I laughed. "Some of them were busy enough trying to miss a bullet."

"But suppose there were one among all those witnesses whose profession it was to take care of motors, one whose ear would note, without conscious effort, the defective firing of a gasoline engine?" Holmes lit a cigarette and walked to the window.

"Hans Behrsin, the chauffeur!" I cried, rushing to the table on which lay the record of the testimony. Hastily running through the index for the chauffeur of Mr. Slater, I found the page where his testimony began and read rapidly and excitedly his description of the murder car as it passed him on Pearl Street at the start of the get-away. The check-up came on page 328 in the middle of a paragraph.

"*It wasn't going very fast,*" I read. "*I do not think

*the car was in good order, anyway!"* Holmes turned
and smiled.

"You see." There was a dramatic pause, after which
I suggested another example.

"Very much like the chance remark of Madeiros'
fellow lodger in Providence that the young Portuguese first became interested in locking his door about
the middle of April, 1920."

"Not quite. Possibly that incident might have been
invented. It is hardly conceivable, however, that
Weeks had read the record of the trial in the Charlestown State Prison anticipating a surprise visit by Mr.
Thompson. And if he had, he would never have lifted
that line out of thousands of pages of testimony. Our
little test is invulnerable.

"Before proceeding further," Holmes continued,
"let us consider the nature of the attack made upon
the Madeiros story. For this purpose I select the argument of Mr. Ranney, the Assistant District Attorney. Obviously, he was in the best position to tear
it down and his familiarity with the evidence made
him a better judge of what was fair than those who
denounced Madeiros in later proceedings. The others
I leave to you."

In his brief filed with the Supreme Judicial Court
in support of Judge Thayer's denial of our motion
for a new trial, Mr. Ranney offered the following
in behalf of the reasonableness of the decision:

"Madeiros has twice been convicted of murder. He

admitted in his deposition that his affidavit, the very cornerstone of this motion, was false in certain particulars. He was unable to remember even the most prominent landmarks at South Braintree. He said that the money stolen was in a black bag, when, as a matter of fact, it was in two steel cases. He said that all of the weapons used were of 38-calibre, when there was no dispute that all the bullets removed from the bodies of the two deceased were of 32-calibre. Under cross-examination he was unable to remember the date of the shooting, a failure of memory appearing also in the affidavits of Dr. Cohoon and of Dr. Thomas. There was evidence also that in the fall of 1925, before December 7, 1925, he said to his sister, Mrs. Matthews: 'You think I am tough because I am in this case. Well, there is a fellow in here over five years who killed two men in a job.' "

[It may be noticed in passing that Mr. Ranney made no attempt then, nor has anyone at any time, to explain the astounding mass of circumstantial evidence implicating the Morellis, nor how Madeiros could invent a lie that squared at every angle with the frame-work of the case against them.]

"Will you comment, my dear Watson?" Holmes suggested. Whereupon, I began as follows:

"It is true that Madeiros was twice convicted of murder, but the statement is without significance. If we are to believe the evidence, he endeavored to communicate with Sacco before his first conviction. When he wrote his confession on the celebrated slip of paper, he was awaiting the outcome of a bill of exceptions to the Supreme Judicial Court. So injurious to Madeiros was this statement regarded at the time that Mr. Ranney, Mr. Thompson, and Mr. Squires—Madeiros' lawyer—agreed to keep it quiet until the appellate court had decided. And then Madeiros was granted a second trial."

"Most significant," said Holmes, touching the tips of his fingers together, "is the fact that after he was granted a new trial, when he stood again innocent until proven guilty and in an infinitely better position than Sacco and Vanzetti, he confirmed without qualification his part in the South Braintree crime to the two physicians mentioned by Mr. Ranney in affidavits produced by the State."

"As to the alleged falsehoods in Madeiros' earlier statement," I continued, "it is obvious that at first Madeiros thought he could confess his own complicity without involving the Morellis. He admitted to Mr. Ranney and the alienists that the names he gave to his two oldest companions were not true. In his prior statement he claimed he was met in Providence by four Italians, but in his deposition he admitted that one of the four—the driver—was a Pole or Finn. Originally he said that he had been picked up at his lodging house, but later that it was a saloon across the street, 'figure it's the same thing.' He also admitted that the addresses of the gangsters as given to Mr.

Thompson were false. In view of Madeiros' expressed attitude that he was 'trying to shield a crowd,' this sort of thing was to be expected whether or not he had been in South Braintree."

"You might add," suggested Holmes, "that Madeiros should be tested by what he claimed was true and not by what he admitted was false."

"Now as to his failure to remember the prominent landmarks at South Braintree," I resumed, "if he was seated, as he said he was, in the rear seat, the curtains down, he would not have observed them—and we do not need to add that he was a half-drunk epileptic, greatly excited at the dangerous game. His general impression, however, was correct, 'there were houses there. I don't know how thickly populated it was. It was not country.' "

"You are not placing yourself in Madeiros' position," interrupted Holmes. "The man on the rear seat of that car would observe many things that happened although it is unlikely that he would have noticed landmarks so obvious to the witnesses on the street, familiar with South Braintree. And bear in mind that, according to the opening of the District Attorney, there was a man on the rear seat as described by Madeiros."

I caught enthusiastically at the idea. "Madeiros' description of the happening of events at the scene of the crime, so far as they could be observed by an occupant of the rear seat, was quite accurate—the stop of the motor car below the spot where the robbery occurred, the number of robbers on the street and in the car, the shots, the boarding of the moving car, the dumping of the loot into the tonneau and the getaway."

"Hear, hear," approved Holmes, "and you might add that he repeatedly corrected Mr. Ranney as the Assistant District Attorney endeavored to lead him into an erroneous description. Listen to the deposition." Holmes then began to read from the record:

"Q.  Five men in the car at the time the shooting took place?

"A.  Five men in the car.

"Q.  Who was doing the shooting?

"A.  *Two men* doing the shooting.

"Q.  Where were they in the car?

"A.  *They were out of the car.*

"Q.  That made seven in the car at the immediate scene of the crime?

"A.  *There were five of us.*

"Q.  How many men were in the car when the two men who you say did the shooting were outside?

"A.  *There was two men in the car.* [Madeiros and the driver.]"

"Madeiros' figures were quite correct. A few seconds later he again avoids a pitfall:

"Q.  Is it fair to say that the men who did the shooting ran to your car and jumped in?

"A.  *While the car was moving.*"

"At this point Madeiros makes the most interesting correction of all, because it pertains to a physical feature of the landscape which could be detected from the inside of the car without looking through the curtains:

"Q. Was the street at that particular point a level street or was it graded?

"A. I think there was a little slope.

"Q. Did you go down grade after the shooting occurred?

"A. *Up grade.*' "

"Madeiros was quite exact—there was a little slope and the car went up grade. Now will you resume your comments?" said Holmes.

"Turning to the use of the phrase 'black bag,' I find that the metal money boxes were of the size and shape of suitcases, dark in color, with handles. One of the government witnesses at the trial had used the same descriptive phrase and, as we later learned, so had witnesses at the inquest. According to Madeiros, the booty was thrown in the tonneau, covered with a blanket and that was the last he saw of it. His wrong guess as to the calibre of the weapons carried by his associates is of no consequence whatsoever, as he had previously stated that he didn't recall what weapons they had, and took no particular notice of them."

"Ah," said Holmes, "Madeiros did not have the benefit of my training in observation."

"Moreover," I continued, "if he had even begun the reading of the record, he would have known that the bullets extracted from the bodies of the dead men were of thirty-two and not of thirty-eight calibre."

"The inductive method," added Holmes, "would also tell you that if Madeiros had seen the testimony he would not have missed the prominent landmarks so frequently mentioned by the eye-witnesses. Remember this, when you come to deal with Judge Thayer's statement that when the Madeiros account tallied he was merely trying to fit his story to the testimony in the case.

"Madeiros' bad memory for dates has already been mentioned. In addition to being unable to recall the date of the shooting, under Mr. Ranney's questioning, he failed to recall many other dates. It was not argued, however, that the other lapses proved the events had not happened. Among other failures of recollection, he could not recall when he finished school; whether he was in his home city of New Bedford in 1919 or 1918; when he committed the act for which he was sentenced in 1920; whether he returned from the south in 1922 or 1923; when he built the garage in back of his house; when he was arrested in Providence for the Wrentham murder; when he was visited by his mother and sister; or when he was visited by the two alienists. Apparently bad memories ran in the Madeiros family because Mr. Ranney filed an affidavit that Madeiros' sister, Mrs. Matthews, could not recall what year she had lived in Providence although it was conceded that she had made her home there for months.

"That disposes of the matter of the date," observed Holmes, "and you need not comment again upon the alleged remark about being 'tough'. The statement, if made, might mean nothing more than a clumsy attempt to cheer up his mother. But in view of Madeiros' denial, and Mrs. Matthews' known twistings in order to create an alibi for him, the supposed remark is hardly a safe foundation to build upon. Have we now finished with Mr. Ranney's direct attack upon the credibility of Madeiros?"

I nodded.

"Very well, then," continued Holmes, "we have now cleared the way for a few real tests of the Madeiros story. Let us suppose that you were Madeiros in prison and wished to build up a lie to the effect that you were present at the South Braintree crime and one of the participants. How would you proceed?"

"I would get the record in the case, learn the principal features of the affair and try to tell a story based on what I had read."

"Exactly. You would build upon the stories told by witnesses and your detail would be the facts reported by them. You would see the crime through the eyes of others, and you would report what they had seen. Therefore, your tale would be simply a composite of the statements of casual witnesses. It would not turn about yourself at all. Has Madeiros done this?"

"Obviously not. It was one of the main grounds for attacking Madeiros that he did not repeat the kind of testimony given by the trial witnesses. Yet, as we have just seen, Madeiros, when pressed, gave a version of the actual crime which was quite correct from the viewpoint of a man sitting in the bandit car behind the lowered curtains."

"Good," said Holmes, "now listen carefully to the story of Madeiros, so different in its details and emphasis from anything related at the trial. He told about making the acquaintance of a gang of criminals in Providence and listening to their tales of crime and profit as related in the local saloons; he remembers the early-morning call at the nearby bar-room—the existence of this saloon was established—the ride at dawn to the saloon in South Boston—also established —to obtain advance information; the killing of time by riding around in the Hudson and visiting speakeasies; the meeting with the Buick car in the Randolph woods three and one-half miles from South Braintree; the exchange of cars; the arrival of the Buick at the scene of the crime; the bandits in the car and on the streets; the shots, the bad start of the car; the boarding of the moving vehicle by the street bandits; the throwing in of the money container and covering it with a blanket; the exchange back again at Randolph; the stop for information as the car left the wild reaches of the Oak Street road. Although Madeiros was then well launched on his criminal career, he was only eighteen years old at the time; this was big stuff for him and he was assigned the relatively minor job of staying in the car to keep back the crowd 'if there was a rush.' One would expect his own emotions to impress themselves on his memory and so they did. At one time he says, 'I was half scared to death,' and on several occasions referred to 'the condition I was in.' The entire story revolves around Madeiros and what he did—not what happened to Parmenter and Berardelli. It has the ring of truth."

After this narration, Holmes remained silent for a few moments, contemplating the cheerful blaze in the fireplace.

"Watson," he finally began, "have you ever considered the persistent perversity of the prosecuting type of mind? Invariably it will test a story according to its similarities with other accounts, whereas the true touchstone of truth is the difference, not the resemblance. Any liar may repeat the testimony of others, but to strike out with new facts—ah, there is the ordeal of truth!" Holmes took a volume of the record from the table.

"Consider, my dear Watson, such a little incident as the stop for information which I have just mentioned in my brief summary of Madeiros' story. There was something new, something not mentioned by any witness at the trial, the occurrence at the fork of Oak and Orchard Streets, in Randolph, just before the Boston Road was reached. Let me read to you Madeiros' account of what happened.

"A.   There was a delay at the fork in the road, and one of the fellows got out and found out from somebody in the house there.

"Q.   What did he want to find out?

"A.   Just which road to take.

"Q.   To get where?

"A.   To go down Providence way.

"Q.   Did you hear the conversation?

"A.   I didn't.

"Q.   Was it a woman?

"A.   I don't know.

"Q.   Did somebody come out of the house or open a window?

"A.   I believe a woman was in the yard; I couldn't see the woman.

"Q.   It was some woman?

"A.   I think it was a woman.

"Q.   Did the car come to a dead stop when this conversation was going on?

"A.   It came to a standstill for a few minutes.

"Q.   I suppose by minutes you might mean seconds?"

"A.   Yes, seconds.

"Q.   Give us as nearly as you can what that conversation was.

"A. There was no conversation. I don't think we were there long enough to have a conversation. He just asked which road went to Providence.

"Q. Which man asked that?

"A. The man in the front seat.

"Q. Was he an Italian?

"A. He was an Italian.

"Q. What did the woman say?

"A. I don't remember.

"Q. What happened after you got your directions?

"A. After we got the directions we went right along, and we went by different roads. They seemed to know the roads after that.

"Q. I want to call to your attention to the front yard of this woman's house where you came to a standstill. After she had told the man who was driving how to get on the Boston road, what did he do?

"A. He backed up just a little and swung around."

"Now mark how the account checked with the actual fact. Mr. Thompson went to the house at this fork and found the lady, a Mrs. Hewins. He was astonished to find that she had been held for two days as a witness for the prosecution at the trial but had never been put on the stand. When she told him that the driver of the murder car was Sacco, however, he understood why she had not been allowed to testify. The prosecution had already put forward a witness who claimed that Vanzetti was the driver, and he in

turn had been overwhelmed by other government witnesses who described the pale, light-complexioned
youth as the chauffeur. If Mrs. Hewins had then testified that Sacco was steering the car, the Government's
case might have gone up in laughter. This lady told
Mr. Thompson that the so-called murder car was
driven rapidly into her yard, apparently uncertain
which way to turn, and then backed out and turned
to the right to go toward the so-called Boston road.
Mr. Thompson took no notes of what she said but recalled that she stated she was either at the open
window or at the door, heard them talking about the
right way to turn, but he did not remember whether
they asked or received any information from her. Mr.
Thompson's statement was not in any way disputed
and was adopted by Mr. Ranney as 'favorable to the
Commonwealth,' presumably"—here Holmes chuckled again—"because of the unique triple threat at
the wheel!"

"The Governor's commission suggested that Madeiros may have heard of the incident."

"It is true that Madeiros lived for a few weeks in
Oak Street vicinity some four and a half years after
the crime," said Holmes, "and the explanation is a
possible one. The significant thing, however, is that
Madeiros has added a new fact which upon investigation proves to be true. It fits perfectly with all the
other pieces in the picture puzzle and its importance
should not be overlooked."

"There is another and even more vital contribution of Madeiros," continued Holmes, "to which I alluded in my brief narrative. I refer now to the exchange of cars in the Oak Street woods. No witness at the trial even hinted at such a happening, and the entire theory of the case was that the bandit car made a continuous escape from South Braintree until it was seen by the last witness at Matfield crossing. If Madeiros is telling the truth, then considerable time must have been lost by the bandits in their flight. The exchange of cars, transfer of booty, switching of number-plates, and scouting necessary for a safe-re-entry upon the road would account for an appreciable delay. If there was no such loss of time, then Madeiros is lying; but if it appears that the bandits' flight did sustain a substantial interruption, then the touchstone has yielded the truth."

"We did not think of that," I admitted reluctantly.

"Ah, Watson," replied Holmes, "sometimes I begin to doubt whether you have learned anything from our association. Fortunately, the reasoning did occur to James E. King, an editor of the *Boston Transcript*, who made a most exhaustive investigation of the subject.[1] And happily for Mr. King's study, he

---

[1] In his letter of July 19, 1927, to the Governor's Advisory Commission, Mr. King says in part:

" . . . fully presuming a strong Commonwealth case, and acting, at the time, upon an editorial purpose highly adverse to the defendants, I began, in regard to the grave matters which your honorable board now is considering, a study which conscience and circumstance have

was aided by the fact that the departure of the murder car from South Braintree and its last appearance at Matfield crossing were both marked by the arrival of trains. From the official train records Mr. King was able to obtain the exact time when these trains passed through the two places. Allowing the escaping car a speed of twenty-five miles an hour, which is generously low in view of the testimony of witnesses along the escape route, Mr. King calculated a delay of *nineteen minutes* between South Braintree and Matfield. Taking the latest time given by any witnesses for the departure from South Braintree, there was a delay of about *twelve minutes*."

Holmes lit another cigarette and lay back blowing rings at the ceiling. I waited for him to resume.

"I have read every word of the record, and have listened to every suggestion, and I say that there isn't even a tenable speculation to explain this curious circumstance, except the story of Madeiros. And I say, further, that any attempt to explain on other grounds, however fantastic, misses the essential point that there was a new fact, offered by Madeiros, unsuspected by anyone connected with the case, which upon investi-

---

impelled me ever since to continue, night and day for more than three months. . . .

"The sources from which I have secured these facts are the New York, New Haven and Hartford's train-sheets for April 15, 1920, two odometer and six chartometer readings of the length of the roads of escape, and a precise study of all statements made by witnesses as to the times when they observed the fleeing criminals and as to the speed at which the fugitives then were proceeding."

gation proves to be true. The fellow must have had intimate knowledge of the crime.

"So, Watson," said Holmes, "the hours pass and I must save my strength for a little encounter tomorrow with the resourceful Moriarty. One more example, however, before we leave Madeiros and his story. In my short summary I mentioned that Madeiros claimed that two cars were used in the crime. He stated that during the escape the Buick was exchanged for a Hudson in the Randolph woods. Here again is a beautiful test, since the trial proceeded upon the theory that only one car was used. Let me call your attention to the fact that the witnesses at the trial apparently shared this view and that practically all of them were subject to the suggestion that the seven-passenger Buick exhibited at the trial was the automobile which they had seen. Judge Thayer also seemed to share this impression. Nevertheless, what do we find when we examine the testimony of witnesses who saw the car after it left Oak Street woods? None of them testified positively that the car which he saw was a Buick. Only one of them, Farmer, thought it was a seven-passenger car; Lloyd and Reed said it was a five-passenger car; and those who noticed its condition described it as old or dirty or both. But this description fits not the Buick, which was a fairly new car; and is inconsistent with the weight of the testimony at the trial as to the type and appearance of the car in South Braintree. And one of the post-Randolph witnesses thought that the car which he had seen might have been a Hudson! Here again we have a new fact contributed by Madeiros, which is substantially checked only by a most careful rereading of the evidence. What do you say now?"

"I am impressed, but not wholly convinced," I replied. "Madeiros says that there were two cars used, a Buick and a Hudson. As proof of this statement you offer the descriptions of confused witnesses."

"Quite right," laughed Holmes. "I wondered whether you would turn my own arguments against me."

"Of course," I said, "if you had any evidence that there actually were two cars cooperating on the crime, then the contribution of Madeiros would be unanswerable."

"I hoped that you would say that," replied Holmes. "Really, Watson, you are progressing." Holmes then went to the table and lifted therefrom a volume of typewritten testimony.

"This is the transcript of the inquest into the deaths of Parmenter and Berardelli. The testimony was given under oath two days after the murders and more than two weeks before Sacco and Vanzetti were arrested. It was kept secret until the summer of 1927, nearly two years after Madeiros made his statement. Please look at the testimony of Shelly Neal, the expressman. You may recall that at the trial thirteen months later he described only one car, a newly varnished Buick, which he saw in the morning when he carried the payroll money into the office and again in the afternoon as the car fled the scene of the crime."

Holmes then handed the volume to me. Hastily turning to Mr. Neal's testimony I read in black and white the confirmation of Madeiros. For it appeared that at the inquest Mr. Neal stated that he did not notice the make of the shiny car which at the trial he stated was a Buick. He described the "newly varnished" car, however, and then reports another car about twenty feet away, which he could not describe but thought "was either dirty color or had not been washed." Neal had to pass between the two cars as he carried the payroll from the train into his office across the street. There was one man in each car. "These two men, as I opened the door, I heard one man say, 'All right,' and I knew that there was conversation between them. As I went through the door a stranger was standing in the entry. . . . " Neal then described the man, generally agreed upon as the driver of the murder car, as "either a Swede or a Finn." When Neal returned to the sidewalk "both cars started very nearly the same time in opposite directions."

Holmes noted my surprise and elation.

"If you will now turn to the testimony of Treacy at the same inquest, you will find further confirmation. Treacy did not testify at the trial."

I did so, and found Neal's account verified by this second witness.

"But why did Neal omit this testimony at the trial?" I inquired.

"The peculiarities of the evidence at the trial are fascinating objects of speculation, but quite irrelevant to our little talk this evening. And now, my dear Watson," said Holmes, arising with a suggestion of finality, "I trust that you will admit that I had good reason for my faith in that fellow Madeiros. Observe that I have not even considered the astounding mass of corroboration which you gathered affecting the Morelli gang. That I shall leave to you. It is now growing quite late and I must get a few hours sleep before encountering that Prince of Evil, old Moriarty, in the morning."

# CHAPTER TEN

## "NONE SO BLIND—"

THE EVIDENCE we had gathered was destined never to be presented before a jury. Of course, the jury which convicted Sacco and Vanzetti in 1921 had no knowledge of the facts incriminating the Morelli gang. Nor did any person, except the New Bedford police, suspect them until after the Madeiros confession in 1926. Few people today know the chain of circumstances linking the Morellis to the South Braintree killings. As will be seen, Governor Fuller took no interest in it, the committee which he appointed misunderstood and omitted much of it, the Supreme Judicial Court of Massachusetts ruled that it had no power to determine the question. There was, in fact, only one judicial hearing—if it may be called that— at which the evidence supporting the Madeiros-Morelli theory was considered at length. This was the hearing at Dedham in September, 1926, upon our motion for a new trial based upon the newly discovered evidence. The denial of this motion effectually ended all real hope of saving Sacco and Vanzetti. Also, it shut off forever any official investigation into the possible guilt of the Morellis.

According to rule of court our motion had to be presented before the judge who had presided over the trial of Sacco and Vanzetti. That judge was Webster Thayer. Judge Thayer had presided over Vanzetti's trial at Plymouth for attempted highway robbery as well as at Dedham where Sacco and Vanzetti were convicted of murder. He had, moreover, already denied numerous previous motions for a new trial. Moreover, he had revealed even at that time an unfriendly attitude toward Sacco and Vanzetti. We knew that he had been quoted as freely expressing his opinion of the guilt of the defendants, his hostility to them as anarchists and Reds, his contempt for their lawyers, and his intention to use his charge to answer the arguments of the defendants' counsel. We did not, however, then know his extreme emotional state concerning Sacco and Vanzetti and we honestly believed that the sheer weight of our evidence would carry Judge Thayer, however unwilling. It was not until nearly a year later that men like Professor James P. Richardson of Dartmouth and Robert Benchley, the writer, volunteered testimony which indicated the Judge's violent hatred of these "anarchistic bastards" and an intention to "get them."

On September 13, 1926, Mr. Thompson began the task of presenting the Madeiros-Morelli evidence before Judge Thayer. At the same time he argued a motion based upon the conceded cooperation of Department officials with the county prosecutor's office. Those who were in the little Dedham courtroom listened to one of the most eloquent and overwhelming pleas in the history of advocacy. Even one of the State detectives, engaged in the business of gathering evidence against Sacco and Vanzetti, was heard to remark, "I'd believe Mr. Thompson had the goods if I didn't know better." Mr. Ranney, the Assistant District Attorney, made little effort to deal with the mass of facts presented by Mr. Thompson, but dwelt chiefly on Madeiros' unreliability and on evidence previously in the case, notably the expert testimony. There were times when Mr. Thompson passed beyond the rôle of lawyer and took his place in history beside the great champions of human rights and liberties. Such a moment occurred in rebuttal when he exclaimed, "and I will say to Your Honor that a government which has come to value its own secrets more than it does the lives of its citizens has become a tyranny, whether you call it a republic, a monarchy, or anything else. Secrets! Secrets!"

Judge Thayer listened impassively to the arguments, which lasted five days. He was uniformly courteous and engaged in an occasional pleasantry. To me it seemed that he must be affected by the succession of undisputed and related facts as unfolded in Mr. Thompson's argument. Within a few weeks I was to learn how completely useless all of our efforts had been.

On October 23, 1926, in a decision which denounced Mr. Thompson as suffering from some form of insanity and charged in substance that Madeiros had been corrupted, Judge Thayer denied the motions for a new trial. He devoted pages in defense of the verdict of the jury and his own conduct of the trial, neither one of which had been challenged by our motions or Mr. Thompson's argument. In justification of the verdict, he even went so far as to quote testimony alleged to have been given by Sacco and Vanzetti at the trial which had never occurred and was in conflict with the record. Even such an event as the surreptitious opening of cartridges by the jury after the evidence had been closed at the Plymouth trial of Vanzetti, which certainly Judge Thayer would ordinarily have condemned, was now stated as if it were a proper occurrence in open court during the trial of the murder cases in Dedham. Expressions and arguments were attributed to Mr. Thompson which he did not use, and action taken by the District Attorney was charged to him in order to add color to the insinuation of a corrupt bargain with Madeiros.

It must not be supposed that Judge Thayer was not sincere or that he was not convinced of the guilt of Sacco and Vanzetti. Nor should it be doubted that he honestly believed he performed a painful duty according to the highest judicial standards and interpreted the evidence in a fair and impartial manner. The explanation of what occurred may be sought in the testimony of unimpeachable witnesses to the effect that Judge Thayer was laboring under the emotions of a passionate advocacy. It has been suggested that this attitude was the result of his belief in the guilt of the men. A belief in the guilt of defendants, however, is a common incident of judicial life and does not stir judges to the point of cursing the men they try or of confusing the evidence.

In the Madeiros-Morelli motion Judge Thayer set himself two questions to answer: "First, what is the character, reputation and record of Madeiros? Second, is he telling the truth or the probable truth on material matters involved in the motion?" It is to be observed he did not ask the question as to how far the evidence, independent of Madeiros' statements, tended to indicate the guilt of the Morelli gang. Nor did he answer it. Replying to the first question which he had prepared, Judge Thayer properly found that Madeiros was very bad. He quite naturally concluded that "an affidavit from a man of this type must be examined and scrutinized with the greatest possible care." But from what type of man would such an affidavit have come with more inherent probability of truth? One would scarcely be inclined to believe a confession from the Bishop of Massachusetts that he was in the murder car, half-drunk, associated with the notorious Morellis in a payroll robbery. The crime itself called for participants who were very bad—as bad as Madeiros.

The decision then proceeded to prove that Madeiros was lying. Part of the proof consisted in adopting the arguments advanced by Mr. Ranney which have already been considered. These included the early falsehoods of Madeiros, his failure to recall landmarks in South Braintree, the mistaken guess as to calibre of the weapons of his associates of which he had taken "no particular notice," [1] and his use of the phrase "black bag" to describe what was thrown into the car. The decision also insinuated that Madeiros was corrupted by reading the financial report of the Sacco-Vanzetti committee which showed a vast sum of money spent—but nothing left—and disputed Madeiros' statement that two cars were used in the escape. We have already seen that this argument was based upon a misconception of the testimony. In fairness to Judge Thayer, however, it should be stated again that neither the record of the inquest, revealing the presence of two cars in South Braintree, nor the time study of Mr. King were then available.

Most of the attack upon Madeiros, however, consisted of an entirely original contribution, unfore-

[1] To Judge Thayer this error "would seem to be almost conclusive against his confession in regard to the Morelli gang.' Had Madeiros been trying to fit his story to evidence given at the trial, which he was accused of doing by Judge Thayer when his statements were correct, he could not possibly have missed the calibre of the bullets that killed Parmenter and Berardelli.

seen by Mr. Ranney in his argument and never
adopted by any subsequent tribunal. This method of
discrediting the story of Madeiros might be termed
"The Test of the Multiplying Italians." This performance required slight changes in the testimony.
These the report proceeded to make so neatly that
only the informed eye could catch the transition.
Once the substitutions were made, however, Judge
Thayer was able to handle the Morelli brothers as a
magician does eggs, producing several from one, and
making the same egg seem to appear in two places
at the same instant.

The starting point was an erroneous parenthetical
statement by Weeks, the pal of Madeiros, namely,
that Fred Morelli was commonly called "Butsy." Mr.
Richards, in commenting on Weeks' affidavit, repeated
the error, but later corrected it. There was no doubt,
however, that it was Frank Morelli who was Butsy.
The testimony given at the Morelli trial in 1920 was
introduced showing from the lips of members of the
gang that Frank was Butsy. Other affidavits confirmed
it. We called attention to Weeks' error in our brief
and in argument before Judge Thayer, and Mr. Ranney conceded that Frank was Butsy, not Fred. Weeks
had further stated:

"Madeiros gave me the names of at least four of
the gang who were in the South Braintree job. I am
sure that the names he gave me were Mike, Joe, Bill
and Butsy. I have an impression that he also men-

tioned Frank, but I am not sure of that. I think he did not mention the name of Patsy as being in that job."

The decision substituted the word "Fred" in the foregoing statement for the word "Butsy." This assumption, false in fact, proved Madeiros a liar, because Fred Morelli, as has been related, was the only brother who was in jail on April 15, 1920. The decision then made a further change by substituting the words "in the murder car" for Weeks' language, "in that job." Nowhere did Weeks relate any statement by Madeiros as to who was "in the murder car." Relying upon these two misquotations of the evidence, Judge Thayer then proceeded with the test.

Madeiros in his deposition claimed there were three Italians in the car along with the driver who was a Swede or a Pole, and Madeiros. We had urged on the court that the three Italians in the car were Joe and Frank Morelli, and Tony Mancini. Mike, we claimed the evidence indicated, had brought the second car from New Bedford and had remained in the Randolph woods when the crime was being committed. However, by making two people out of Butsy—Fred and Frank—Judge Thayer got four Italians into the car and, by the second change in Weeks' statement, added Mike for good measure, making five Italians in addition to Madeiros and the driver.

However, the decision not only expanded one Italian into two, when occasion required, but also con-

tracted two into one. Originally Madeiros had stated
that the leader of the gang, and the oldest, was called
"Mike." He said at the time that the names did not
"amount to anything," later admitted that they were
wrong, and that Joe Morelli was older than Mike
Morelli. He admitted that he had been trying to
"shield a crowd." The real Mike Morelli lived in
New Bedford and was a petty criminal compared
with his older brother, Joe, the notorious head of the
Morelli gang in Providence. We had urged that the
"old man" who, according to Madeiros, had planned
and directed the South Braintree crime, was Joe, the
real boss, and that the real Mike Morelli had taken
charge of the murder car in Randolph, returning with
it to New Bedford after the crime, where it was seen
by Sergeant Jacobs. Judge Thayer provisionally accepted our contention that Mike Morelli was in charge
of the Buick seen by Sergeant Jacobs in New Bedford.
He rejected, however, all of the evidence indicating
that Joe was the leader originally called "Mike" by
Madeiros, and assumed that the "old man" was intended by Madeiros to be Joe's obscure, younger
brother, Mike. Of course, if Mike was driving a Buick
in New Bedford between five and five-thirty P. M. on
the afternoon of the crime, he could hardly have returned to Providence with the others in the Hudson
car. This, according to the decision, established a
"pretty good alibi" for Mike. This "alibi", however,
rested upon the supposition that "Mike Morelli was

the leader of the gang"—which he was not. One can almost hear the redoubtable Joe sniff his contempt at the suggestion that he and Mike were the same person.

The decision also stressed the fact that "sixty cents were found on the front seat of the abandoned Buick car, in the Manley woods." This seemed to indicate to the Judge that there had been a hurried division of the spoils in which the change was dropped, and if there was such a scramble, Madeiros must have seen the money boxes. The suggestion implies that the criminals, instead of removing the boxes from the murder car, remained in the car while they pried open the steel boxes, broke into the "wooden boxes" contained therein, and then tore open the hundreds of pay envelopes in each of which "was the exact amount due each employee." Such a proceeding would stamp as half-wits the men who planned and executed the South Braintree crime. Moreover, the "sixty cents" was not found on the front seat, but "under the back edge of the front seat on the . . . right along on the wood with the cover of the tool box." Most drivers of cars would assume that the change had slipped from some trouser pocket and worked under the seat rather than that it had escaped during a supposed frantic and complicated operation of dividing more than fifteen thousand dollars in loot.

Such reasons for denying the Madeiros-Morelli motion may be compared with the evidence which Judge Thayer ignored or forgot. If Madeiros con-

cocted a false story in his cell at Dedham, then what
possible explanation can be offered for the amazing
series of undisputed corroborative facts unfolded by
a private and inexpert investigation? Silence is the
answer given in the decision and silence has been the
only explanation ever offered. A story is told by a
robber in the Dedham jail concerning a crime which
occurred nearly six years before. It throws suspicion
upon a gang of criminals, active and at liberty at
the time, facing large expenditures for counsel fees
and bail because of pending Federal indictments
against them. It appears that shortly before the crime
the gang suddenly appeared in possession of a car of
the same type and make as the murder car and that
the car disappeared immediately thereafter. The number-plates on the car next appear on the gang's Cole
8. The New Bedford police suspect the Morellis of
the South Braintree crime at the time and members
of the gang when confronted by Sergeant Jacobs in
Fiore's restaurant, act as if they are ready for serious
trouble. The "mob" consists chiefly of Italians, as
described at the trial, and the car containing the
murderers, when last seen, is headed in the general
direction of their headquarters in Providence. The
Morellis are American-born and therefore capable of
speaking "clear and unmistakable" English to this last
witness of their flight—a feat impossible for Vanzetti to whom the language was attributed.

It further appears that the gang spotted shipments

of merchandise in the factory so that these might be
later stolen from the freight cars and that of nine
counts for stolen shoes, five were for shipments from
Rice and Hutchins and Slater and Morrill at South
Braintree. A spotter could not help but note the arrival of the payroll and the manner in which it was
handled. Thus the story told in Dedham leads straight
to the very spot on which the paymaster and guard
were shot to death.

Suspicion against one dangerous member of the
gang is confirmed by Joe Morelli's outburst in Leavenworth to "see Mancini about that." Mancini's record
disclosed the fact that he is as cool a murderer as ever
lived, just the type required for the systematic killing
of two men before a hundred eyes in South Braintree. Then the record of his weapon indicates that
it was of very peculiar make and calibre, described
by experts years before as the requisite for the gun
which fired five bullets into the bodies of Berardelli
and Parmenter, and left three of the four shells produced at the trial. As for the other bullet and shell,
if they were fired by a Colt thirty-two, it appears
from the record of the Morelli trial in 1920 that Joe
had several such weapons. According to Madeiros,
the oldest of the Italians was about forty years of age
and the next oldest thirty-five. In fact, Joe Morelli
was then in his thirty-ninth year, and Tony Mancini
in his thirty-fourth.

And then comes the last ironic touch to this confession, assumed to be a lie. Not only do Joe Morelli and Tony Mancini correspond to Sacco in height and weight, but nature had stamped Joe with features so strikingly similar to those of Sacco that even government witnesses exclaimed, on seeing the photograph, "That's the man." Of course, if the two men were placed side by side, differences would be obvious, but to persons who saw the murderer for a few seconds only, the resemblances would be overwhelming.

When confronted with the possibility of being accused of the South Braintree crimes, the members of the Morelli gang, represented by counsel, lie so lustily that on their own contradictions they would be held in an ordinary case. The lying begins in Fiore's restaurant a few days after the crime; it is resumed to the laughing point six years later. Yet, if innocent, the Morellis, unlike Sacco and Vanzetti, had nothing to fear.

On these things and their irresistible implications, the decision is silent. Likewise, certain general considerations passed unnoticed. The Madeiros-Morelli evidence did not contain the great gaps which existed in the case against Sacco and Vanzetti. All of the participants were accounted for, not merely two; all of the shots, not merely one. The link between the criminals and South Braintree was securely forged and not left to tenuous speculation. It supplied the solid motive of professionals in grave need of money in place of the corridor insinuations, each of which was disproved, concerning Sacco and Vanzetti. Above all, it presented men trained in the planning of crime and capable of carrying out any brutal enterprise, whereas the other case called on one to believe that the perpetrators were a shoemaker and a fish peddler, men who had borne good reputations prior to their arrest, hard working and industrious, giving their spare time to agitation in behalf of their fellow workers. "But this Court, if his natural feelings of humanity were stretched to the limit, cannot find as a fact that Madeiros told the truth." Judge Thayer denied the motion for a new trial.

The next step was the Supreme Judicial Court. On January 27 and 28, 1927, our exceptions were argued before the highest Appellate Court in the Commonwealth. I had expected Mr. Thompson to make the entire argument but during the first morning recess he told me that his voice was tiring and asked me to continue while he rested. I have always suspected the sufficiency of his excuse because it was characteristic of him to desire me to receive more credit than I deserved. How far my performance met his standards I do not know, but it was the easiest argument I have ever made, as I was saturated with the facts. We alternated for two days and then waited anxiously for the outcome. As the younger and less experienced man, I had hopes which Mr. Thompson sustained. What he really thought, however, I learned by accident one day when he mistook me for his partner, Mr. George

Mears, as I entered the room. "There's no hope," he said hoarsely, "no hope." He was quite right.

On April 5, the Supreme Judicial Court overruled our exceptions. Following the doctrine laid down in a civil case, the Court held that "it is not imperative that a new trial be granted even though the evidence is newly discovered, and, if presented to a jury, would justify a different verdict." The Court then held that it had no jurisdiction to decide the matter except to determine whether Judge Thayer had acted "conscientiously, intelligently and honestly."

"We have considered carefully the helpful and minute discussion contained in the brief and the argument for the defendants. We have studied the numerous affidavits, exhibits and records placed before us and the statements of the decision in the light of all the arguments of counsel for defendants. It is not necessary to discuss them in detail. As already stated, it is not for us to determine what is to be believed. The question for us is: Could the judge conscientiously, intelligently and honestly have reached the result he has reached? As stated in *Davis* v. *Boston Elevated Railway*, supra, at page 502, 'To sustain these exceptions it is necessary to decide that no conscientious judge, acting intelligently, could honestly have taken the view expressed by him.' "

The mere statement of such a rigid rule contains its own answer. The Court could not say that the Judge was neither conscientious, intelligent, nor honest. Such a judge would be "justified" in finding that the evidence which we offered concerning the Morellis fell "far short of furnishing adequate proofs of their guilt or of establishing reasonable doubt of the guilt of the defendants." The word "justified" is here used in its technical sense to mean that such a finding could be supported, but did not necessarily represent the conclusion which the Supreme Judicial Court might have reached on the same evidence. As if to indicate its own aloofness fom the finding on the Morelli evidence, the opinion, in the next paragraph, dealing with the Department of Justice collaboration, indicated its complete agreement with Judge Thayer by using the words, "He would be compelled to find, etc. . . . "

Partisans on both sides have claimed that the Supreme Judicial Court did not give its true reasons. One group maintains that the Court believed the men guilty and therefore refused to interfere; another group that the Court felt that it was more important to save the face of the great trial court than to save Sacco and Vanzetti; the radical element that it was a mere class decision. It is safer, however, to take the Court at its word rather than to speculate. Certainly the doctrine which it enforced was not invented for the Sacco-Vanzetti case, but had its origin in a civil suit decided years before. The decision, however, revealed a lack of power in the appellate court to correct injustices in important criminal cases. Thereupon, to provide

against similar situations in the future, the Judicial
Council and the Attorney-General urged upon the next
session of the Legislature that "the functions of the
Supreme Judicial Court on appeal be so broadened
that it will be empowered to pass upon the whole
case, including questions of law or fact, and will have
power to order a new trial upon any ground if the
interest of justice appear to require it." This is the
New York rule and not dissimilar from the English
practice. The Judicial Council and the Attorney-General's office are the two bodies in the Commonwealth
charged with recommending improvement in the administration of justice. Nevertheless, so strong was
the feeling in Massachusetts against Sacco and Vanzetti, then dead for six months, that a few loud and
absurd shouts from persons having no responsibility
blocked this highly desirable and civilized legislative
proposal. To label anything "Sacco-Vanzetti propa-
ganda" was a blight sufficient to wither any measure
in the Legislature of Massachusetts in the year 1928.

After the decision of the Supreme Judicial Court,
Judge Thayer sentenced Sacco and Vanzetti to death.
The episode proved to be one of the most moving
incidents in judicial history. The eloquence of Vanzetti's broken English, coupled with a moderation
born of seven years' agony, produced a tragic inver-
sion of the situation, so that Vanzetti assumed to be
the judge and his sentencer the culprit. When he
concluded, there were tears in the eyes of practically

everyone, including the District Attorney for Norfolk County and his assistants. Thereafter the case was borne on a constantly rising tide of excitement to its fatal culmination on August 22, 1927.

The appeal to Governor Alvan T. Fuller was signed by Vanzetti alone; Sacco refused to sign on the ground that it was against his principles to make futile gestures toward a capitalist tribunal. Meanwhile, groups of citizens began to petition the Governor to appoint a commission to aid him in his investigation, and he responded by appointing A. Lawrence Lowell, President of Harvard University, S. W. Stratton, President of the Massachusetts Institute of Technology, and Robert Grant, a novelist and former judge of the Probate Court. It is my opinion that the adverse reports of these men did more to make the death of Sacco and Vanzetti acceptable to a doubting world than any decision of judge or jury. And yet these men had no special training in weighing evidence. Moreover, their policy was not to interview any persons who had already testified or filed affidavits, and very few such witnesses or affiants came before them. Therefore, their opportunity of forming judgments was not necessarily greater than that of eminent jurists who studied the record and followed the case— and arrived at entirely different conclusions.

Moreover, on the score of time alone the commission attempted an impossible task. Properly to digest a record of thousands of pages, interview many

persons, conduct hearings of the many witnesses who
had not appeared during the judicial proceedings, and
some who had, demanded leisure and deliberation.
Yet, according to the Governor, "they began work as
soon as their other affairs could be arranged, labored
continuously during much of June and through
July. . . ." As a matter of fact, June witnessed the
extensive graduation exercises in both of the univer-
sities whose heads sat on the commission, and their
report was completed on July 27, 1927. Working at
high speed in the hottest summer weather, it is not
surprising that the report shows the effects of cramming and haste.

The personnel of the Committee was almost
wholly unsatisfactory to us as counsel for the men.
One of the appointments was protested in our behalf
by Mr. John F. Moors, an eminent and courageous
citizen of Boston, on the ground that this member of
the commission had already expressed himself vio-
lently against Sacco and Vanzetti. The protest produced neither substitution nor resignation. Another
member would never have been acceptable to us because reports seemed to indicate that he lacked the
sturdy independence necessary to withstand the flood
of pressure demanding the death of our clients. The
remaining appointee would have been approved by us
on his known contacts and independence. Even as to
this member, however, we felt that his life had been
an alternation of ventures in the highest liberalism

and the narrowest prejudice, so that it was a gamble as to which mood would conquer. We had not proceeded many days before the Committee, however, when it became apparent that our solitary hope had made up his mind and that evidence and argument were utterly useless. Mr. Thompson and I then decided to take the drastic step of refusing to go on before the commission. The doom of our clients seemed as inevitable as that of Socrates, and we were unwilling to continue in the farce of fair treatment. We were diverted from this course, however, by two outstanding jurists, closely connected with Harvard affairs, who inspired us with some semblance of hope. Theirs was perhaps the greater wisdom, since, had we withdrawn, it would have been said that we had lost faith in the cause of our clients.

The Committee did not permit us to be present during their interviews with Judge Thayer, Chief Justice Hall, the eleven surviving jurors of the Dedham trial, and Mr. Katzmann, the District Attorney who tried the case. We were, however, allowed to question Mr. Katzmann later. Nor were we allowed to participate in "what came incidentally in an inspection of the scene of the murder and a visit to Sacco, Vanzetti and Madeiros in prison." So far as we know, we were present during the examinations of all other witnesses, but the hearings, against our protest, were entirely private. The reason given for such privacy was that witnesses would be more apt to speak freely if they thought that what they said would not be published by the press. However, all but two of these witnesses were for the defense and we wanted no such protection for them. The two witnesses for the prosecution were an obviously unbalanced individual, who craved publicity, and her employer.

It is my purpose to discuss the Committee's report only so far as it bears on the Madeiros-Morelli evidence. Other aspects have been competently dealt with by others, including Professor John Dewey in *The New Republic* (issue of November 23, 1927) and Osmond K. Fraenkel in his scholarly work, *The Sacco-Vanzetti Case*. The report consists of about twenty printed pages, two of which deal with the Madeiros-Morelli evidence, yet those two pages contain such strange misconceptions that these cannot wholly be attributed to mental indigestion brought on by cramming.

"The impression has gone abroad that Madeiros confessed committing the murder at South Braintree. Strangely enough, this is not really the case. He confesses to being present, but not to being guilty of the murder. That is, he says that he, as a youth of eighteen, was induced to go with the others without knowing where he was going or what was to be done, save that there was to be a hold-up which would not involve killing; and that he took no part in what was done. In short, if he were tried, his own confession, if wholly believed, would not be sufficient for a verdict of murder in the first degree."

This statement is wholly incorrect. The law of Massachusetts is clear and to the contrary. It is first degree murder to participate in a robbery where a killing results, whether the murder was originally intended or not, and no matter who does the slaying. Only a few months before the Committee wrote this statement there had occurred in Boston the triple execution of the so-called carbarn bandits, only one of whom had killed the watchman in a surprise encounter while his companions were in another part of the building, stealing the money. Though this statement might be laid to a startling ignorance of the law, what explanation can be given for the perfect comprehension when dealing with the evidence against Vanzetti? "Under these circumstances, if he was with Sacco, or in the bandits' car, or indeed *in South Braintree at all that day,* he was undoubtedly guilty." Then, discussing the rather unsatisfactory identification evidence against Vanzetti, the report concludes, *"He was evidently not in the foreground.* On the whole, we are of the opinion that *Vanzetti also was guilty beyond a reasonable doubt."* There was no claim nor evidence produced that Vanzetti had fired any of the shots. The report therefore means that Madeiros, if he were in the murder car holding a pistol to prevent a rush while his confederates shot the paymaster and his guard, was not guilty of murder, whereas Vanzetti, if he were in South Braintree at all, was guilty beyond a reasonable doubt. Such confusion of mind is perhaps indicative of the spirit of the Committee.

The report continues in regard to Madeiros: "His ignorance of what happened is extraordinary, and much of it cannot be attributed to a desire to shield his associates, for it had no connection therewith. This is true of his inability to recollect the position of the buildings, and whether one or more men were killed. In his deposition he says that he was so scared that he could remember nothing immediately after the shooting. To the Committee he said that the shooting brought on an epileptic fit which showed itself by a failure of memory; but that hardly explains the fact that he could not tell the Committee whether before the shooting the car reached its position in front of the Slater & Morrill factory by going down Pearl Street or by a circuit through a roundabout road."

The statement does not mention the fact that Madeiros did suffer from epilepsy and poor memory, and that if, as he said, he sat in the rear seat with curtains drawn—there was such a man described in the District Attorney's opening to the jury—then there was no particular reason why he would have noted landmarks or the route of the car before the shooting. Madeiros claimed he had never been to South Braintree before the crime or after; his claim was not contradicted but seemed confirmed by his very inability to describe the position of the buildings. "Indeed, in

his whole testimony there is only one fact that can be
checked up as showing a personal knowledge of what
really happened, and that was his statement that after
the murder the car stopped to ask the way at the house
of Mrs. Hewins at the corner of Oak and Orchard
Streets in Randolph. As this house was not far from
the place on a nearby road where Madeiros subsequently lived, he might very well have heard the fact
mentioned."

From this statement no reader would guess that
Madeiros had accurately described in detail the
sequence of events at the scene of the crime. As has
been seen, he depicted correctly the stop of the motor
car below the scene of the robbery, the number of robbers in the street and in the car, the shots, the boarding of the moving car, the dumping of the loot in the
tonneau and the escape. Particularly interesting were
his replies to Mr. Ranney's efforts to lead him into
misstating the details. Madeiros had continually corrected him, ending with this rather remarkable evidence of knowledge:

"Q. Did you go down grade after the shooting
occurred?

"A. Up grade."

Of course, these were matters which could be
observed from a position within the car and did not
involve staring out of the drawn curtains. The report
does not mention that Madeiros' statement that there
were two cars involved in the crime, instead of one as

was supposed, was partially corroborated by the inquest testimony produced. His account of the halt in
the Randolph woods is discussed in another part of
the report. The incident in front of the Hewins' house
had never been testified to by anyone except Madeiros,
so the committee disposes of it by pure guessing—
"He might very well have heard the fact mentioned."
This is not the only place where the Committee nulli-
fies favorable evidence by preferring to speculate on
what might have happened instead of accepting the
record. In one instance, unrelated to Madeiros, the
Committee apparently relied upon the last margin of
possibility to meet an especially strong line of Vanzetti's defense "that no ticket that could be used was
sold that morning at any of the stations in or near
Plymouth, and that no such cash fare was paid or
mileage book punched, but that does not exhaust the
possibilities." The Committee had stated that one question to be answered by them was whether Sacco and
Vanzetti were guilty beyond a reasonable doubt.
"Reasonable doubt" was apparently removed by the
process of rejecting embarrassing evidence in favor of
"exhausting the possibilities."

However, the Committee did not entirely ignore
the Morelli evidence as Judge Thayer had done.
"How far do the other affidavits corroborate his statement? They state that Madeiros—who seems to have
been rather prone to boast of his feats—had previously told Weeks that he had taken part with the Mo-

relli gang in the South Braintree crime, and had talked with the Monterios also about it. The affidavits further state that he was acquainted with this gang, which consisted of a hardened set of criminals who had stolen shoes shipped from the Slater & Morrill and Rice & Hutchins factories, and were accustomed to spot the shipments when made at such factories; that on April 15th, 1920, a number of that gang were out on bail for a different offense for which they were afterwards sentenced, and consequently could physically have been at South Braintree; that the photographs of Joe Morelli showed a distinct resemblance to Sacco and to whoever shot Berardelli, and that of Benkoski to the driver of the car—but identification by photograph is very uncertain; that Joe Morelli possessed a Colt automatic thirty-two caliber pistol. They state that one of the gang was seen in Providence late on the afternoon of April 15th in a Buick car which, by the officer who so reported, was seen no more. In regard to the last item, the great improbability may be noted that bandits who intended to hide the car in which they made their escape should have first shown it in the streets of Providence after all but one of the members of the gang had already returned in another car. Even without considering the contradictory evidence it does not seem to the Committee that these affidavits to corroborate a worthless confession are of such weight as to deserve serious attention."

It is to be observed that the report suggests a new

explanation for Madeiros' confession—"boastfulness." Certainly, Madeiros' actions during his brief lifetime had spoken louder than words. Mr. Ranney had called him a "psychopathic personality" and Judge Thayer had charged corruption. Governor Fuller will offer the most bizarre of all explanations. Meanwhile no one assumes, even tentatively, that he is telling the truth.

This attempted summary of the Morelli evidence is the most extended notice that it ever received from any tribunal. The error in stating that the Buick was seen in Providence, instead of New Bedford, is of great significance and will be considered later. The summary, however, omits the Mancini pistol and its startling relation to shots and shells; Joe Morelli's slip to "see Mancini about that"; the fact that the Buick had suddenly appeared in Mike Morelli's possession shortly before the crime; the incident of the number-plates and Fiore's restaurant; the suspicions of the New Bedford police against the Morellis in 1920; and the inexplicable lies of the Morellis in the presence of their own counsel and in affidavits taken by him. Of course, none of the large implications of the Madeiros-Morelli evidence is even suggested by the report.

Incomplete and inaccurate as the summary is, however, one may query why the Committee did not wonder how a falsehood in the Dedham jail could lead so directly to a set of criminals of the kind de-

scribed at the trial, available to commit the crime and
riveted to the fatal spot in South Braintree by indisputable records. The answer is suggested by the passage quoted. The confession was "worthless," therefore the affidavits did not "deserve serious attention."
The reasoning is curious and contrary to normal
human judgments. Suppose a prospector of poor reputation told an unlikely story of finding gold in a certain locality. Assume that a group of amateurs went
to the region and returned with nuggets of gold found
on the spot. Is it conceivable that a committee appointed to investigate would report that the nuggets
were not worth serious attention because the prospector's story was worthless?

The admission that the Committee did not pay
serious attention to the Morelli evidence explains
why the members failed to draw any inferences from
it. The misstatement that the Buick car was seen in
Providence instead of New Bedford is really of pro-
found significance. It represents not merely a careless
reading of the evidence, but indicates a complete
failure to understand the criminal technique exhibited
in the Morelli evidence. No one who understood the
Morelli theory could have been guilty of such a mistake. The report, building on the error, says "the great
improbability may be noted that the bandits who intended to hide the car in which they made their escape
should have first shown it in the streets of Providence,
etc." The Committee refuses to believe such folly of

the Morellis. They do believe, however, the theory
of the prosecution, that after committing murder and
robbery, Sacco, Vanzetti and their companions drove
the automobile through the environs of West Bridgewater, where it was alleged they had their headquarters and garage, and then abandoned the murder car
in the woods, less than two miles away. The recon-
ciliation of these beliefs is a problem for the psy-
chologists. Finally the report creates the impression
that the evidence which it attempted to summarize was
contradicted by some other evidence—"Even without
considering the contradictory evidence." None of the
propositions in the summary was contradicted by evidence—unless the denials by the Morellis be so regarded. Most of them were buttressed by records in
various courts, police and prosecutors' offices, and
could not be refuted.

This is the entire reference in the report on the
Madeiros-Morelli evidence except for a passage dealing with the King investigation. "Mr. James E. King
brought to the attention of the Committee some calculations he has been making about the position at various
times of the escaping bandit car, to the effect that if it
travelled at the rate of speed the witnesses testified it
would have taken much more [2] time than elapsed between the moment of the murder and the arrival at the
Matfield crossing. He suggested that the delay could

[2] Obviously an error as the sense calls for "less," not "more,"—an
inadvertence doubtless due to hasty composition.

be accounted for on the theory that the Morelli gang had committed the murder and spent some time in the Randolph woods three and a half miles from South Braintree while changing from a Buick to a Hudson, as described by Madeiros. To the Committee it seems that the calculations are based upon somewhat uncertain data, and that the delay is apparently accounted for by the undisputed fact that the bandits turned by mistake into Orchard Street, which leads into a much-travelled highway and to the town of Randolph; that discovering their mistake, they retraced their steps and inquired at the Hewins house the way to the old turnpike. It seems incredible that the bandits, as Mr. King supposes, should have spent something like twenty minutes in woods not far from the road and so short a distance from the scene of the murder."

Of course, as has been seen, Mr. King's study was important confirmation of Madeiros since, until the confession, it had been supposed by everyone that the escape was continuous. It was Madeiros who told of the trick of exchanging cars in the Randolph woods. The explanation offered by the Committee is hopelessly inadequate. The Hewins incident is told by Madeiros, and by Mrs. Hewins through Mr. Thompson's affidavit. Both versions agree in substance, namely, that there was a brief pause in the fork opposite Mrs. Hewins' house, that an inquiry was made, that the car backed and continued its course. There was no "retracing their steps" as suggested, unless by this is meant that the car was backed for the turn. But even if the car had travelled the entire length of Orchard Street and returned, the distance is too short to account for any substantial delay. In discussing this incident, Mr. Fraenkel, in his book on the Sacco-Vanzetti case, confirms my own experience that such an operation would consume about four minutes. Mr. King's careful work, therefore, remains unexplained except by Madeiros.

It seems incredible to the Committee that the bandits should have exchanged cars in the woods not far from the road and so short a distance from the scene of the crime. The road was lonely and screened by scrub oak, the region sparsely populated even as late as 1926, when I first saw it. The device of exchanging cars had to be employed near the scene of the crime or else it served no purpose. The idea was for the bandits to escape, unnoticed, in a car of entirely different appearance. This would have been defeated had they placed the point of exchange too far away. Moreover "twenty minutes" was Mr. King's highest estimate of the duration of the delay. What seems unbelievable to the Committee seemed natural to a local paper, *The Brockton Enterprise*, on the day after the murder, which reported that the police were working on this "incredible" theory.

The Committee was composed of men who had no known familiarity whatsoever with professional criminal technique. It probably also seemed incredible to them that the escaping bandit car should speed south toward Holbrook out of South Braintree, and then double back on a hairpin turn into the very town where they had committed murder. Yet such was the fact, and the ruse was so successful that police and pursuers were piled up in Holbrook while the bandits passed through the lonely Oak Street woods in Randolph. It would seem scarcely possible that the crime could have been more thoroughly planned, more accurately timed, or neatly executed. Yet the report closes with characteristic assurance: "It has been urged that a crime of this kind must have been committed by professionals, and it is for well-known criminal gangs that one must look; but to the Committee both this crime and the one at Bridgewater do not seem to bear the marks of professionals, but of men inexpert in such crimes."

No reasons are given for such an opinion. It certainly did not represent the view of Captain Proctor, veteran head of the State police, who was removed from the case by the District Attorney, nor that of older men in the Department of Justice. Such an expression, however, gives rise to wonder why two college presidents and a retired Probate Judge should assume to be experts in matters so remote from their own experience and knowledge.

Meanwhile Governor Alvan T. Fuller was conducting his own investigation, in his own way. The method was to interview witnesses secretly in what history long ago characterized as "star chamber" proceedings. Mr. Thompson repeatedly thundered his objections to the process, pointing out that the experience of mankind demonstrated that such tactics did not conduce to the truth. The Governor, who had begun business as a bicycle rider and had become a millionaire automobile distributor, was one of those financially successful men who apparently held in contempt lawyers and all their works. If we were allowed to be present while the Governor sought the truth from witnesses, his office would be turned into a "bear den." It is true that he was attended by his personal counsel, Mr. Joseph H. Wiggin, but it was impossible for this lawyer to know the complicated record as we knew it or to represent at once the interest of the prosecution and the defense. Moreover, from what we observed and what was reported to us, the Governor persisted in plunging ahead with little restraint or guidance from Mr. Wiggin.

The Governor sent for many witnesses. We read their names in the newspapers. He also permitted us to suggest witnesses and then sent for them, but we were not allowed to be present. We had no knowledge of what was said to the Governor except as he may have casually repeated it to us during our several conferences or as some of our witnesses may have reported later. These gleanings indicated a situation which any trained lawyer could have anticipated.

Witnesses, unchecked, told stories which varied from their sworn testimony in open court. Others, with bits of evidence important only if connected with other facts, were not allowed to proceed because the Governor was not interested in what seemed to him to be irrelevant. Others were so erroneously presented to the Governor by his secretary that the entire bearing of the testimony was lost or distorted. We also learned later that communications of the utmost importance, which Mr. Thompson and I sent to the Governor, were held up by this same secretary. Getting evidence to the Governor reminded one of Lincoln's observation that sending troops to the Army of the Potomac was "like shoveling fleas across a barn door, half of them never got there."

For example, the Governor, in his talks with us and in his report, quite properly laid stress on the Bridgewater case. If Vanzetti were guilty in that attempted hold-up, then he was capable of participating in the South Braintree affair. The Governor cited to us a witness who, he said, positively identified Vanzetti as one of the bandits. I called his attention to the fact that this witness had been uncertain at the trial when he was under oath. The Governor then said that the witness had received a threatening letter.[3]

When I reminded him that this same man had expressed doubt at the preliminary hearing on May 15,

---

[3] This may be compared with the statement in his report, "clear-eyed witnesses, unafraid to tell the truth."

1920, nine days after the arrest and years before the alleged threat had been received, the Governor did not answer. How much other testimony of the same type the Governor received and believed we do not know. As a matter of fact, the "Pinkerton reports" so-called, made available to us in the summer of 1927, smashed the Bridgewater identification evidence against Vanzetti upon which the Governor relied. This detective agency had represented the company which had insured the payroll, and their operators began to investigate immediately after the attempt, on December 24, 1919. Promptly upon receiving these reports Mr. Thompson and I analyzed their contents in a long memorandum which we sent to the Governor. Three weeks later Mr. John F. Moors was discussing the case with the Governor who again emphasized the Bridgewater matter. According to Mr. Moors, the latter asked whether the Governor had given heed to certain reports of the Pinkerton detectives; the Governor turned to his secretary and asked him whether or not he knew anything about some Pinkerton reports; his secretary paused for a moment and then said something about a "cropped mustache."

The same chaotic condition was reported to us by Mr. Richards of Providence. At our request, Mr. Richards had been sent for as an informed person who could tell the Governor about the various members of the Morelli gang. As soon as he started the subject, however, the Governor, according to Mr.

Richards, stopped him by remarking that he did not care to know about it, but that he wanted to learn what Mr. Richards knew of this South Braintree murder. As Mr. Richards knew nothing of the shooting of Parmenter and Berardelli, he was dismissed without telling his story. Fresh from this interview, Mr. Richards told us that our clients were as good as dead, that the Governor neither knew nor cared to know anything about the Madeiros evidence.

We have the Governor's own statement that Mr. Richards was quite correct. Shortly after Vanzetti's petition reached the Governor's office, Mr. Fuller was reported in the Boston press as stating that he put no credence in Madeiros. Also, he was quoted by Robert Lincoln O'Brien, then editor of the *Boston Herald,* as stating that "he cared nothing about Madeiros and his confession."

This attitude toward the Madeiros confession, expressed at the outset of the investigation, was confirmed in the Governor's report of August 3, 1927. "I give no weight to the Madeiros confession. It is popularly supposed he confessed to committing this crime. In his testimony to me he could not recall the details or describe the neighborhood. He furthermore stated that the Government had doublecrossed him and he proposes to doublecross the Government. He feels that the District Attorney's office has treated him unfairly because his two confederates who were associated with him in the commission of the murder for which he was convicted were given life sentences, whereas he was sentenced to death. He confessed the crime for which he was convicted. I am not impressed with his knowledge of the South Braintree murders."

The reason here put forward to explain Madeiros' confession is certainly novel—to punish the Government! "Psychopathic," says the District Attorney; "corruption" says the Judge; "vainglory" says the commission; "revenge" says the Governor. Not one suggests the simple explanation offered by Madeiros, "maybe it's true." Of all the intimations, that of the Governor is most interesting. Possibly a professional criminal would understand that the State had a special interest in seeing that Sacco and Vanzetti remained convicted and that pain would be inflicted upon the authorities by asserting that he and the Morelli gang were guilty. I rather think, however, that such thoughts were quite foreign to the world of Madeiros. It is far more likely that the idea was attributed to Madeiros by one who lived in an atmosphere which identified the interest of the State with the electrocution of Sacco and Vanzetti. We shall see in a moment who brought up this subject of "double-crossing." How much time was devoted by the Governor in discussing with Madeiros the South Braintree crime and how much was devoted to the alleged feeling against the District Attorney? The *Boston Traveler* for July 22, 1927, reports that the entire interview lasted fifteen minutes. Meanwhile, it is to be observed that the Gov-

ernor makes no mention whatever of the Madeiros-
Morelli evidence.

Fortunately for the history of the case we have
Madeiros' version of his interview with Governor
Fuller. It is related by Mr. Thompson on the witness
stand in the case of *Commonwealth* v. *Harry J.
Canter*. Mr. Thompson talked with Madeiros on Au-
gust 4, 1927, at the State Prison.

"Madeiros said that Governor Fuller had come
down to see him and that the Governor began the interview by saying that he understood that Madeiros
said that he thought he had been given—I think the
expression was, 'a raw deal,' or something indicating
double-dealing, or improper dealing by the Government, and that Madeiros said that Officer Ferrari of
the State police had given him a promise of second
degree murder if he confessed the murder, and that
was given to Mr. Brooks who was employed at the
State House and who had a good deal to do with
criminal cases. The Governor said if he was satisfied
that any such promise had been made he would do
something for Madeiros. The Governor then said,
before waiting for any reply from Madeiros, according to Madeiros' statement to me, 'You do not know
anything about the Sacco-Vanzetti case, do you?'
And Madeiros said he did, and the Governor asked
him if he was in the car with the other men who committed the murder in South Braintree, the South
Braintree murder, and Madeiros said that he was,

and the Governor then said, 'So you are a double murderer; I will do nothing for you.' "

The implication in the Madeiros version makes unpleasant reading. And yet, poor as his reputation for truth-telling may have been, Madeiros, when he related the incident, was in the death-house, with no hope of escaping electrocution. Mr. Thompson was not his lawyer and could do nothing for him. The story, in the main, is corroborated by the Governor's own statement. Perhaps some future Da Vinci will paint the scene suggested by Madeiros. The artist will place his characters in the death-house at Charlestown, although at the time of the Governor's visit the transfer had not yet been made. In the background, through an open door, are seen several figures working over the electric chair, a portion of which is visible from the cell-block. In the immediate foreground is the cell of Vanzetti and through the bars we can see that he is reading—probably *The Rise of American Civilization* by Charles and Mary Beard, which he studied up to the hour of his death. Just beyond is Sacco, writing, perhaps the memorable letter to his son, Dante, to whom he bequeathed the beauty of nature and love for the weak and helpless. In the center, flanked by a uniformed escort, stands the perfectly groomed Governor of Massachusetts smiling blandly at someone in the cage before him. Contrasting strangely with this embodiment of success and power, slouches the figure of Madeiros, doomed, hopeless, and worm-eaten from birth. Yet the genius has depicted upon the face peering through the steel bars an expression of surprise changing to contempt as the friendless epileptic from the Azores realizes that the great Governor is merely trying to sell him a bill of goods for a recantation. And perhaps in a subtle way the artist may transmit the thought that Madeiros will spurn the proferred traffic, preferring Sacco, Vanzetti, the chair and the truth.

# APPENDIX

# CHRONOLOGY†

1919
November 22nd,       Theft of Buick car in Needham.
*December 5th,       *Morellis indicted for freight car robberies.*

December 22nd,       Theft of number plates used at Bridgewater.

December 24th,       Attempted hold-up in Bridgewater.

1920
January       Theft of number plates used at South Braintree.

*March 5th,       *New indictment of Morellis for freight car robberies.*

*April —       *"Mike" Morelli seen with Buick in New Bedford.*

*April 15th,       *"Mike" Morelli's Buick seen for last time in New Bedford.*

April 15th,       Murders at South Braintree.
April 17th,       Inquest at Quincy with regard to these murders.

April 17th,       Discovery of Buick car in Manley woods.

* The additions of the author have been marked with an asterisk.
† Reprinted from Osmond K. Fraenkel's *The Sacco-Vanzetti Case* by the courtesy of the publishers, Alfred A. Knopf, New York, N. Y.

| April 20th, | Interview of Boda by Police. |
| *April 24th, | *Incident at Fiore's restaurant, New Bedford.* |
| April 25th, | Vanzetti's trip to New York. |
| April 29th, | Vanzetti's return to Plymouth. |
| *May 1st, | *Madeiros' first arrest in New Bedford.* |
| May 2nd, | Meeting in Boston of Sacco, Vanzetti and others. |
| May 3d, | Death in New York of Salsedo. |
| May 5th, | Visit of Sacco, Vanzetti, Boda and Orciani to Johnson house, followed by arrest of Sacco and Vanzetti. |
| May 6th, | Arrest of Orciani. |
| May 6th, | Interview of Sacco and Vanzetti by District Attorney Katzmann. |
| *May 11th to May 25th, | *Trial at Providence of Morelli gang on Federal indictments.* |
| May 18th, | Preliminary hearing against Vanzetti in relation to the Bridgewater case. |
| *May 25th, | *Madeiros' second arrest in New Bedford.* |
| May 26th, | Preliminary hearing at Brockton against Sacco. |
| *June 3rd, | *Sentence of members of Morelli gang to U. S. Penitentiary.* |
| June 11th, | Indictment of Vanzetti for Bridgewater hold-up. |
| *June 14th, | *Madeiros sentenced to five months in House of Correction.* |
| June 22nd to July 1st, | Trial at Plymouth of Vanzetti for Bridgewater hold-up. |
| August 16th, | Sentence of Vanzetti for Bridgewater hold-up. |

September 11th,    Indictment of Sacco and Van-
                   zetti for South Braintree murders.

1921
*January,          *Madeiros goes south with ap-
                   proximately $2800.*
*February 10th,    *Mancini murders Alterio on
                   Mulberry Street, New York.*
May 31st to July 14th,  Trial of Sacco and Vanzetti at
                   Dedham.
November 5th,      Motion for new trial as against
                   the weight of evidence argued
                   before Judge Thayer.
November 8th,      First supplementary motion filed
                   (Ripley).
*December 21st,    *Sentence of Mancini on plea of
                   guilty in New York.*
December 24th,     Motion for new trial as against
                   the weight of evidence denied.

1922
May 4th,           Second supplementary motion
                   filed (Gould and Pelser).
July 22nd,         Third supplementary motion
                   filed (Goodridge).
September 11th,    Fourth supplementary motion
                   filed (Andrews).

1923
April 30th,        Fifth supplementary motion filed
                   (Hamilton).
October 1st,       Supplement to first motion filed
                   (Daly).
October 1st to 3rd,     ⎧All five supplementary motions
November 1st, 2nd, 8th, ⎨argued before Judge Thayer.
November 5th,           ⎩Proctor motion filed.

1924
October 1st,       Decisions by Judge Thayer deny-
                   ing all motions.

| | |
|---|---|
| *November 1st, | *Madeiros kills cashier at Wrentham bank.* |
| *November 17th, | *Madeiros arrested in Providence.* |

**1925**

| | |
|---|---|
| *May 11th, | *First trial of Madeiros at Dedham.* |
| *November 16th, | *First written confession by Madeiros.* |
| November 18th, | Madeiros statement received by Sacco in Dedham prison. |

**1926**

| | |
|---|---|
| January 11th to 13th, | Argument of appeal of Sacco and Vanzetti from conviction and from denial of first, second and fifth supplementary motions. |
| March 31st, | Conviction of Madeiros reversed by Supreme Judicial Court. |
| May 12th, | Conviction of Sacco and Vanzetti affirmed by Supreme Judicial Court. |
| May 15th to May 20th, | Second trial of Madeiros. |
| *May 22nd, | *Investigation of Madeiros story begun by Mr. Thompson and Mr. Ehrmann.* |
| May 26th, | Motion based on Madeiros' statement filed. |
| September 13th to 17th, | Madeiros motion argued before Judge Thayer. |
| October 23rd, | Decision by Judge Thayer denying motion. |

**1927**

| | |
|---|---|
| January 27th and 28th, | Appeal from Denial of Madeiros' motion argued before Supreme Judicial Court. |

| | |
|---|---|
| April 5th, | Denial of motion affirmed. |
| April 9th, | Sentence imposed by Judge Thayer on Sacco and Vanzetti. |
| May 3rd, | Petition for clemency addressed to Gov. Fuller. |
| June 1st, | Advisory Committee appointed by Gov. Fuller. |
| July 11th to 21st, | Hearings held before Advisory Committee. |
| August 3rd, | Decision by Governor Fuller denying clemency. |
| August 6th, | Motion filed for revocation of sentence. |
| August 6th, | Petition filed for writ of error. |
| August 8th, | Motion denied by Judge Thayer. |
| August 8th, | Petition denied by Judge Sanderson. |
| August 10th, | Petition for writ of habeas corpus denied by Justice Holmes of the United States Supreme Court, and by Judge Anderson of the United States District Court. |
| August 16th, | Exceptions to denial of motion and petition argued in Supreme Judicial Court. |
| August 19th, | Exceptions overruled by Supreme Judicial Court. |
| August 20th, | Petition for writ of habeas corpus denied by Judge Morton of the United States Circuit Court of Appeals. |
| August 20th, | Petition for stay and extension of time in which to apply to the United States Supreme Court for writ of certiorari denied by Justice Holmes of the United States Supreme Court. |

| August 22nd, | Similar petition denied by Justice Stone of the United States Supreme Court. |
| August 23rd, | Sacco and Vanzetti and Madeiros executed. |
| October 3rd, | Petition for writ of certiorari dismissed by consent in the Supreme Court of the United States. |

## Evidence against Sacco and Vanzetti: Compared with evidence against Madeiros-Morellis. (From *Defendant's Brief before Supreme Judicial Court.*)

| | *Madeiros-Morelli* | *Sacco-Vanzetti* |
|---|---|---|
| *Character of accused* | Typical gangsters and gunmen of the worst type. | One of them an industrious workmen with a family and a savings bank deposit, and no previous criminal record. The other a fish peddler never before his arrest accused of crime. Both unpopular as pacifists and extreme radicals. |
| *Motive.* | Desperate need of funds for lawyer and bail before trial for serious Federal offence. Source of income through robbing freight cars blocked by U. S. Marshal and R. R. Police. | Robbery for private gain alleged. No claim or evidence that either defendant ever received or had any part of the stolen money. |
| *Opportunity to plan crime.* | Had been repeatedly stealing large shipments from *Slater and Morrill* and *Rice and Hutchins* of *South Braintree* after a member of the gang had 'spotted' them in that place. | None alleged. |
| *Accusation by confederate* | Direct testimony of participant. | None. |

| | | |
|---|---|---|
| *Identification by others.* | Opportunity restricted, but Joe, Mancini, and Benkosky identified from photographs by Government as well as defense witnesses. No available photographs of Mike or Frank. Undoubted resemblance of Joe Morelli to Sacco in many particulars. | Some identification of Sacco; very slight of Vanzetti at the scene of the murder. Identifications open not only to doubt, but to the gravest suspicion owing to unprecedented manner of displaying these defendants, previous identifications of other criminals by same witnesses, changes in stories, suppression of testimony, manifestly impossible details such as the man identified as Vanzetti using 'clear and unmistakable English,' and the man identified as Sacco having an unusually large hand. |
| *Alibi.* | Full of contradictions as to Morellis. None by Madeiros. | Testified to by many reputable witnesses. |
| *Consciousness of guilt.* | Alleged motion to draw gun on officer—uncontradicted. | Alleged motion to draw gun on officer — contradicted. |
| | Falsehoods consistent with nothing but consciousness of guilt of crime charged. Confession by Madeiros. | Falsehoods explained by terror felt by radicals and draft evaders at time of persecution of 'reds' two days after murder or suicide of a friend [1] while in the custody of Department of Justice officials. |
| *Bullets.* | One fired from pistol of type owned by Joe Morelli (Colt 32), and five from type owned by Mancini ('Star' or 'Steyr', 765 mm.). | One only claimed to have been fired by weapon of Sacco, and none by Vanzetti. Sharp disagreement of experts, but if real opinion of one of the Government's experts had been known at the time of the trial he would have proved a *defence witness*.[2] |

*Other
Corroborative
Matter.*

Morellis were American-born and could have used 'clear and unmistakable' English. *Every member of the m u r d e r p a r t y accounted for.* Unwillingness of Morelli lawyer to state anything tending to implicate his f o r m e r clients in the South Braintree murders.

Testimony shows that cap claimed to be Sacco's was *not* identified by Kelly, and effort to connect Vanzetti's popular make of revolver with Berardelli's supported by most remote type of evidence, including confused records of gun-shop offered by an ex-agent (unrevealed)' of the Department of Justice.[3] Does not account for other members of the party.

*Stolen Money.*

Madeiros' possession of $2,800 immediately thereafter (about his 'split' of the total sum stolen).

None. On the contrary, when arrested, Sacco and Vanzetti, supposed to be in possession of over $15,000, and ex-hypothesi, to be accomplished automobile thieves, were using street cars after an unsuccessful attempt to borrow a friend's [4] six-year-old Overland.

*Attitude of
Authorities.*

Seriously offer statements and affidavits of Morellis denying participation in crime. Declined request of defendant's counsel to interview *all witnesses* jointly to avoid vulgar contest of affidavits. Declined to investigate.

Anti-Red excitement capitalized; highly prejudicial cross-examination as to draft evasion and anarchistic opinions and associations; patriotic speeches and charge by Judge to jury; interference by Department of Justice agents who believed defendants innocent; suppression of testimony favorable to defence; intentionally misleading testimony of experts [5] on vital points."

[1] Salsedo.
[2] Proctor.
[3] Wadsworth.
[4] Boda.
[5] Proctor.

# RECORD OF THE SENTENCING

# OF SACCO AND VANZETTI

## SPEECHES TO THE COURT

*The speeches of Sacco and Vanzetti to Judge Webster Thayer in the Dedham Court House on April 9, 1927, were taken down by court stenographers. The difference between the spelling and punctuation in them and the spelling and punctuation in the letters of the two men is thereby explained.*

CLERK WORTHINGTON: *Nicola Sacco,* have you anything to say why sentence of death should not be passed upon you?

NICOLA SACCO: Yes, sir. I am no orator. It is not very familiar with me the English language, and as I know, as my friend has told me, my comrade Vanzetti will speak more long, so I thought to give him the chance.

I never knew, never heard, even read in history anything so cruel as this Court. After seven years prosecuting they still consider us guilty. And these gentle people here are arrayed with us in this court today.

I know the sentence will be between two classes, the oppressed class and the rich class, and there will be always collision between one and the other. We fraternize the people with the books, with the literature. You persecute the people, tyrannize them and kill them. We try the education of people always. You try to put a path between us and some other nationality that hates each other. That is why I am here today on this bench, for having been of the oppressed class. Well, you are the oppressor.

You know it, Judge Thayer—you know all my life, you know why I have been here, and after seven years that you have been persecuting me and my poor wife, and you still today sentence us to death. I would like to tell all my life, but what is the use? You know all about what I say before, that is, my comrade, will be talking, because he is more familiar with the language, and I will give him a chance. My comrade, the kind man to all the children, you sentenced him two times, in the Bridgewater case and the Dedham case, connected with me, and you know he is innocent.

You forget all this population that has been with us for seven years, to sympathize and give us all their energy and all their kindness. You do not care for them. Among that peoples and the comrades and the working class there is a big legion of intellectual people which have been with us for seven years, to not commit the iniquitous sentence, but still the Court goes ahead. And I want to thank you all, you peoples, my comrades who have been with me for seven years, with the Sacco-Vanzetti case, and I will give my friend a chance.

I forget one thing which my comrade remember me. As I said before, Judge Thayer know all my life, and he know that I am never guilty, never—not yesterday, nor today, nor forever.

CLERK WORTHINGTON: *Bartolomeo Vanzetti*, have you anything to say why sentence of death should not be passed upon you?

BARTOLOMEO VANZETTI: Yes. What I say is that I am innocent, not only of the Braintree crime, but also of the Bridgewater crime. That I am not only innocent of these two crimes, but in all my life I have never stolen and I have never killed and I have never spilled blood. That is what I

want to say. And it is not all. Not only am I innocent of
these two crimes, not only in all my life I have never stolen,
never killed, never spilled blood, but I have struggled all
my life, since I began to reason, to eliminate crime from
the earth.

Everybody that knows these two arms knows very well
that I did not need to go into the streets and kill a man
or try to take money. I can live by my two hands and live
well. But besides that, I can live even without work with
my hands for other people. I have had plenty of chance to
live independently and to live what the world conceives to
be a higher life than to gain our bread with the sweat of our
brow.

My father in Italy is in a good condition. I could have
come back in Italy and he would have welcomed me every
time with open arms. Even if I come back there with not a
cent in my pocket, my father could have give me a position, not to work but to make business, or to oversee upon
the land that he owns. He has wrote me many letters in that
sense, and as another well-to-do relative has wrote me letters in that sense that I can produce.

Well, it may be said to be a boast. My father and my aunt
can boast themselves and say things that people may not be
compelled to believe. People may say they may be poor
when I say that they are in good condition to give me a position any time that I want to settle down and form a family and
start a settled life. Well, but there are people may be in
this same court that could testify to what I have said and
that what my father and my aunt have said to me is not a
lie, that really they have the means to give me a position
any time that I want.

Well, I want to reach a little point farther, and it is this,
that not only have I not been trying to steal in Bridgewater,
not only have I not been in Braintree to steal and kill and
have never stolen or killed or spilt blood in all my life, not
only have I struggled hard against crimes, but I have refused
myself of what are considered the commodity and glories

of life, the prides of a life of a good position, because in my consideration it is not right to exploit man. I have refused to go in business because I understand that business is a speculation on profit upon certain people that must depend upon the business man, and I do not consider that that is right and therefore I refuse to do that.

Now, I should say that I am not only innocent of all these things, not only have I never committed a real crime in my life—though some sins but not crimes—not only have I struggled all my life to eliminate crimes, the crimes that the official law and the moral law condemns, but also the crime that the moral law and the official law sanction and sanctify—the exploitation and the oppression of the man by the man, and if there is a reason why I am here as a guilty man, if there is a reason why you in a few minutes can doom me, it is this reason and none else.

There is the best man I ever cast my eyes upon since I lived, a man that will last and will grow always more near to and more dear to the heart of the people, so long as admiration for goodness, for virtues, and for sacrifice will last. I mean Eugene Victor Debs.

He has said that not even a dog that kills chickens would have found an American jury disposed to convict it with the proof that the Commonwealth has produced against us. That man was not with me in Plymouth or with Sacco where he was on the day of the crime. You can say that it is arbitrary, what we are saying from him, that he is good and he applied to the other his goodness, that he is incapable of crime, and he believed that everybody is incapable of crime.

Well, it may be like that but it is not, it could be like that but it is not, and that man had a real experience of court, of prison and of jury. Just because he wanted the world a little better he was persecuted and slandered from his boyhood youthness to his old age, and indeed he was murdered by the prison.

He knew, and not only he knew, but every man of understanding in the world, not only in this country but also in other countries, men to whom we have provided a certain amount of the records of the case at times, they all know and still stick with us, the flower of mankind of Europe, the better writers, the greatest thinkers of Europe, have pleaded in our favor. The scientists, the greatest scientists, the greatest statesmen of Europe, have pleaded in our favor.

Is it possible that only a few, a handful of men of the jury, only two or three other men, who would shame their mother for worldly honor and for earthly fortune; is it possible that they are right against what the world, for the whole world has said that it is wrong and I know that it is wrong? If there is one that should know it, if it is right or if it is wrong, it is I and this man. You see it is seven years that we are in jail. What we have suffered during these seven years no human tongue can say, and yet you see me before you, not trembling, you see me looking you in your eyes straight, not blushing, not changing color, not ashamed or in fear.

Eugene Debs said that not even a dog—something like that—not even a dog that kill the chickens would have been found guilty by an American jury with the evidence that the Commonwealth have produced against us. I say that not even a leprous dog would have had his appeals refused two times by the Supreme Court of Massachusetts—not even a leprous dog.

They have given a new trial to Madeiros for the reason that the Judge had either forgot or omitted to tell the jury that they should consider the man innocent until found guilty in the court, or something of that sort. That man has confessed. The man was tried on his confession and was found guilty, and the Supreme Court gave him another trial. We have proved that there could not have been another Judge on the face of the earth more prejudiced, more cruel and more hostile than you have been against us. We have proven that. Still they refuse the new trial. We know, and you know in your heart, that you have been against us from the very beginning, before you see us. Before you see us

you already know that we were radicals, that we were under-
dogs, that we were the enemy of the institutions that you can
believe in good faith in their goodness—I don't want to discuss that—and that it was easy at the time of the first trial to
get a verdict of guiltiness.

We know that you have spoken yourself, and have spoke
your hostility against us, and your despisement against us
with friends of yours on the train, at the University Club of
Boston, at the Golf Club of Worcester. I am sure that if
the people who know all what you say against us have the
civil courage to take the stand, maybe your Honor—I am
sorry to say this because you are an old man, and I have
an old father—but maybe you would be beside us in good
justice at this time.

When you sentenced me at the Plymouth trial you say, to
the best of my memory, of my good faith, that crimes were
in accordance with my principle—something of that sort—
and you took off one charge, if I remember it exactly, from
the jury. The jury was so violent against me that they found
me guilty of both charges, because there were only two. But
they would have found me guilty of a dozen of charges
against your Honor's instructions. Of course I remember
that you told them that there was no reason to believe that
if I were the bandit I have intention to kill somebody, so
that they should take off the indictment of attempt to murder. Well, they found me guilty of what? Also of an attempt
to murder. And if I am right, you take out that and sentence
me only for attempt to rob with arms,—something like that.
But, Judge Thayer, you give more to me for that attempt
of robbery than all the 448 men that were in Charlestown,
all of those that attempted to rob, all those that have robbed,
they have not such a sentence as you gave to me for an
attempt at robbery.

I am willing that everybody that does or does not believe
me that they can make commission, they can go over there,
and I am very willing that the people should go over there
and see whether it is true or not. There are people in

Charlestown who are professional robbers, who have been in half the prisons of the United States, that have stolen, or injured men or shot them. Most of them guilty without doubt, by self-confession, and by confession of their own partners, and they got eight to ten, eight to twelve, ten to fifteen. None of them has twelve to fifteen, as you gave me for an attempt at robbery. And besides that, you know that I was not guilty; that I had not been in Bridgewater attempting to steal. You know that my life, my private and public life in Plymouth, and wherever I have been, was so exemplary that one of the worst fears of our prosecutor Katzmann was to introduce proof of our life and of our conduct. He has opposed it with all his might and he has succeeded.

You know that if we would have had Mr. Thompson, or even the brothers McAnarney, in the first trial in Plymouth, you know that no jury would have found me guilty. My first lawyer has been a partner of Mr. Katzmann, as he is still now. The first lawyer of the defense, Mr. Vahey, has not defended me, has sold me for thirty golden money like Judas sold Jesus Christ. If that man has not told to you or to Mr. Katzmann that he knew that I was guilty, it is because he cannot, it is because he knew that I was not guilty. That man has done everything indirectly to hurt us. He has made a long speech to the jury about things that do matter nothing, and on the point of essence to the trial he has passed over with few words or with complete silence. This was a premeditation in order to give to the jury the impression that my own defender has nothing good to urge in defense of myself, and therefore is compelled to go around the bush on little things that amount to nothing and let pass the essential points either in silence or with a very weakly resistance.

We were tried during a time whose character has now passed into history. I mean by that, a time when there was a hysteria of resentment and hate against the people of our principles, against the foreigner, against slackers, and it seems to me—rather, I am positive of it, that both you and

Mr. Katzmann have done all what it were in your power in order to work out, in order to agitate still more the passion of the juror, the prejudice of the juror, against us.

I remember that Mr. Katzmann has introduced a witness against us, a certain Ricci. Well, I have heard that witness. It seems that he has nothing to say. It seemed that it was a foolishness to produce a witness that has nothing to say. And it seemed as if he were called by the Commonwealth to tell to the jury that he was the foreman of those laborers who were near the scene of the crime and who claimed, and who testified in our behalf, that we were not the men, and that this man, the witness Ricci, was their foreman, and he has tried to keep the men on the job instead of going to see what was happening so as to give the impression that it was not true that the men went towards the street to see what happened. But that was not very important. The real importance is what that man said and that was not true, that a certain witness who was the water boy of the gang of the laborers testified that he took a pail and went to a certain spring, a water spring, to take water for the gang—Ricci testified it was not true that that man went to that spring, and therefore it was not true that he saw the bandit, and therefore it was not true that he can tell that neither I nor Sacco were the men. But Ricci was introduced to show that it was not true that that man went to that spring, because he knew that the Germans had poisoned the water in that spring. That is what he, Ricci, said on that stand over there. Now, in the world chronicle of the time there is not a single happening of that nature. Nobody in America—we have read plenty things bad that the Germans have done in Europe during the war, but nobody can prove and nobody will say that the Germans are bad enough to poison the spring water in this country during the war.

Now, this, it seems, has nothing to do with us directly. It seems to be a thing said by incident on the stand between the other things; why, whereas, that is the essence here. Because the jury were hating us because we were against the

war, and the jury don't know that it makes any difference between a man that is against the war because he believes
that the war is unjust, because he hate no country, because
he is a cosmopolitan, and a man that is against the war because he is in favor of the other country that fights against
the country in which he is, and therefore a spy, an enemy,
and he commits any crime in the country in which he is in
behalf of the other country in order to serve the other
country. We are not men of that kind. Nobody can say that
we are German spies or spies of any kind. Katzmann knows
very well that. Katzmann knows that we were against the
war because we did not believe in the purpose for which
they say that the war was fought. We believe that the war
is wrong, and we believe this more now after ten years that
we studied and observed and understood it day by day—
the consequences and the result of the after war. We believe
more now than ever that the war was wrong, and we are
against war more now than ever, and I am glad to be on the
doomed scaffold if I can say to mankind, "Look out; you
are in a catacomb of the flower of mankind. For what? All
that they say to you, all that they have promised to you—it
was a lie, it was an illusion, it was a cheat, it was a fraud,
it was a crime. They promised you liberty. Where is liberty?
They promised you prosperity. Where is prosperity? They
have promised you elevation. Where is the elevation?"

From the day that I went in Charlestown, the misfortunate, the population of Charlestown, has doubled in number.
Where is the moral good that the war has given to the world?
Where is the spiritual progress that we have achieved from
the war? Where are the security of life, the security of the
things that we possess for our necessity? Where are the
respect for human life? Where are the respect and the admiration for the good characteristics and the good of the
human nature? Never before the war as now have there
been so many crimes, so much corruption, so much degen-
eration as there is now.

In the best of my recollection and of my good faith, dur-

ing the trial Katzmann has told to the jury that a certain
Coacci has brought in Italy the money that, according to
the State theory, I and Sacco have stolen in Braintree. We
never stole that money. But Katzmann, when he told that
to the jury, he knew already that that was not true. He knew
already that that man was deported in Italy by the federal
police soon after our arrest. I remember well that I was
told that the federal policeman had him in their possession
—that the federal policeman had taken away the trunks
from the very ship where he was, and brought the trunks
back over here and look them over and found not a single
money.

Now, I call that murder, to tell to the jury that a friend
or comrade or a relative or acquaintance of the charged
man, of the indicted man, has carried the money to Italy,
when he knows it was not true. I can call that nothing else
but murder, a plain murder.

But Katzmann has told something else also against us
that was not true. If I understand well, there have been
agreement of counsel during the trial in which the counsel
of defense shall not produce any evidence of my good conduct in Plymouth and the counsel of the prosecution would
not have let the jury know that I was tried and convicted
another time before in Plymouth. Well, it was masterly called
"a one-sided agreement" by someone very competent. In
fact, even the telephone poles knew at the time of this trial
at Dedham that I was tried and convicted in Plymouth; the
jurymen knew that even when they slept. On the other side
the jury have never seen I or Sacco and I think we have
the right to incline to believe that the jury have never approached before the trial anyone that was sufficiently intimate with me and Sacco to be able to give them a description of our personal conduct. The jury don't know anything
about us. They have never seen us. The only thing that they
know is the bad things that the newspaper have said on the
Plymouth trial.

I don't know why the defense counsel have made such an

agreement but I know very well why Katzmann had made such agreement; because he know that half of the population of Plymouth would have been willing to come over here and say that in seven years that I was living amongst them that I was never seen drunk, that I was known as the most strong and steadfast worker of the community. As a matter of fact I was called a mule and the people that know a little better the condition of my father and that I was a single man, much wondered at me and say, "Why you work like a mad man in that way when you have no children and no wife to care about?"

Well, Katzmann should have been satisfied on that agreement. He could have thanked his God and estimate himself a lucky man. But he was not satisfied with that. He broke his word and he told to the jury that I was tried before; he told it to this very court. I don't know if that is right in the record, if that was taken off or not, but I heard with my ears. When two or three women from Plymouth come to take the stand, the woman reached that point where this gentleman sits over there, the jury were seated in their place, and Katzmann asked these women if they have not testified before for Vanzetti, and they say, yes, and he tell to them, "You cannot testify." They left the room. After that they testified just the same. But in the meanwhile he told the jury that I have been tried before. That I think is not giving justice to the man from one who is looking after the truth, and it is with such insuperable frameups with which he has split my life and doomed me.

It was also said that the defense has put every obstacle to the handling of this case in order to delay the case. That sounds weak for us, and I think it is injurious because it is not true. If we consider that the prosecution, the State, has employed one entire year to prosecute us, that is, one of the five years that the case has lasted was taken by the prosecution to begin our trial, our first trial. Then the defense makes an appeal to you and you waited, for I think that you were resolute, that you had the resolution in your heart from even when the trial finished that you will have refused every appeal that we will put up to you. You waited a month or a month and a half and just lay down your decision on the eve of Christmas—just on the eve of Christmas, eve of Christmas. We do not believe in Christmas, neither in the historical way nor in the church way. But, you know, some of our folks still believe in that, and because we do not believe in that, it don't mean that we are not human. We are human, and Christmas is sweet to the heart of every man. I think that you have done that, to hand down your decision on the eve of Christmas, to poison the heart of our family and of our beloved. I am sorry to be compelled to say this, but everything that was said or done on your side since then has confirmed my suspicion time after time until that suspicion has changed to certitude.

Then the defense, in presenting the new appeal, has not taken more time than you have taken in answer to that. Then there came the second appeal, and now I am not sure whether it is the second appeal or the third appeal where you waited eleven months or one year without an answer to us, and I am sure that you had decided to refuse us a new trial before the hearing for the new appeal began. You took one year to answer it, or eleven months—something like that. So that you see that out of the five years, two were taken by the State from the day of our arrest to the trial, and then one year to wait for your answer on the second or the third appeal.

Then on another occasion that I don't remember exactly now, Mr. Williams was sick and the things were delayed not for fault of the defense but on account of the prosecution. So that I am positive that if a man take a pencil in his hand and compute the time taken by the prosecution in prosecuting the case, and the time that was taken by the defense to defend this case, the prosecution has taken more time than the defense, and there is a great consideration that must be taken in this point, and it is that my first lawyer betrayed us—the whole American population were against us.

We have the misfortune to take a man from California, and he came here, and he was ostracized by you and by every authority, even by the jury, and is so much so that not even Massachusetts is immune from what I could call a universal prejudice—the belief that each people in each place of the world, they believe to be the better of the world, and they believe that all the other people of the other places of the world are not so good as they. So of course the man that came from California into Massachusetts to defend two of us, he must be licked if it is possible, and he was licked all right. And we have our part, too.

What I want to say is this: Everybody ought to understand that the first beginning of our defense has been terrible. My first lawyer did not try to defend us. He has made no attempt to collect witnesses and evidence in our favor. The record in the Plymouth court is a pity. I am told that they are part or almost one-half lost. So that later on the defense have had a tremendous work to do in order to collect some evidence, to collect some testimony to offset and to learn what the testimony of the State had been. And in this consideration it must be said that even if the defense take double time of the State about delays, double time than they (the State) delayed the case, it would have been reasonable just the same, whereas it took less than the State.

Well, I have already say that I not only am not guilty of these two crimes, but I never committed a crime in my life —I have never stolen and I have never killed and I have never spilt blood, and I have fought against crime, and I have fought and I have sacrificed myself even to eliminate the crimes that the law and the church legitimate and sanctify.

This is what I say: I would not wish to a dog or to a snake, to the most low and misfortunate creature of the earth—I would not wish to any of them what I have had to suffer for things that I am not guilty of. I am suffering because I am a radical and indeed I am a radical; I have suffered because I was an Italian, and indeed I am an Italian; I have suffered more for my family and for my beloved than for myself; but I am so convinced to be right that you can only kill me once but if you could execute me two times, and if I could be reborn two other times, I would live again to do what I have done already.

I have finished. Thank you.

THE COURT: Under the law of Massachusetts the jury says whether a defendant is guilty or innocent. The Court has absolutely nothing to do with that question. The law of Massachusetts provides that a Judge cannot deal in any way with the facts. As far as he can go under our law is to state the evidence.

During the trial many exceptions were taken. Those exceptions were taken to the Supreme Judicial Court. That Court, after examining the entire record, after examining all the exceptions—that Court in its final words said, "The verdicts of the jury should stand; exceptions overruled." That being true, there is only one thing that this Court can do. It is not a matter of discretion. It is a matter of statutory requirement, and that being true there is only one duty that now devolves upon this Court, and that is to pronounce the sentence.

First the Court pronounces sentence upon Nicola Sacco:

*It is considered and ordered by the Court that you, Nicola Sacco, suffer the punishment of death by the passage of a current of electricity through your body within the week beginning on Sunday, the tenth day of July, in the Year of our Lord, One Thousand Nine Hundred and Twenty-seven. This is the sentence of the law.*

Then upon Vanzetti:

*It is considered and ordered by the Court that you, Bartolomeo Vanzetti . . .*

VANZETTI: Wait a minute, please, your Honor. May I speak for a minute with my lawyer, Mr. Thompson?

THOMPSON: I do not know what he has to say.

THE COURT: I think I should pronounce the sentence.

*. . . Bartolomeo Vanzetti, suffer the punishment of death . . .*

SACCO: You know I am innocent. Those are the same words I pronounced seven years ago. You condemn two innocent men.

THE COURT: *. . . by the passage of a current of electricity through your body within the week beginning on Sunday, the tenth day of July, in the year of our Lord, One Thousand Nine Hundred and Twenty-seven. This is the sentence of the law.*

*The next day Vanzetti handed to friends the notes of what he had wished to say further to Judge Thayer when he interrupted the pronouncement of sentence. Included in those notes was this estimate of Sacco:*

I have talk a great deal of myself but I even forgot to name Sacco. Sacco too is a worker from his boyhood, a skilled worker lover of work, with a good job and pay, a bank account, a good and lovely wife, two beautiful children and a neat little home at the verge of a wood, near a brook. Sacco is a heart, a faith, a character, a man; a man lover of nature and of mankind. A man who gave all, who sacrifice all to the cause of Liberty and to his love for mankind; money, rest, mundain ambitions, his own wife, his children, himself and his own life. Sacco has never dreamt to steal, never to assassinate. He and I have never brought a morsel of bread to our mouths, from our childhood to to-day—which has not been gained by the sweat of our brows. Never. His people also are in good position and of good reputation.

Oh, yes, I may be more witful, as some have put it, I am a better babbler than he is, but many, many times in hearing his heartful voice ringing a faith sublime, in considering his supreme sacrifice, remembering his heroism I felt small small at the presence of his greatness and found myself compelled to fight back from my eyes the tears, and quanch my heart trobling to my throat to not weep before him—this man called thief and assassin and doomed. But Sacco's name will live in the hearts of the people and in their gratitude when Katzmann's and yours bones will be dispersed by time, when your name, his name, your laws, institutions, and your false god are but a *deem rememoring of a cursed past in which man was wolf to the man.* . . .

# DECISION OF GOVERNOR FULLER

BOSTON, MASSACHUSETTS,
AUGUST 3, 1927

ON APRIL 15th, 1920, a paymaster and his guard were held up, robbed and brutally murdered at South Braintree, Massachusetts. On May 5th, 1920, Nicola Sacco and Bartolomeo Vanzetti were arrested; they were later tried and found guilty of the murder. The verdict was followed by seven motions for a new trial and two appeals to the Supreme Court for the Commonwealth, all of which were heard and later denied. Prior to the trial of the two men in this case, Vanzetti had been arrested, tried and convicted of an attempted holdup on December 24, 1919, at Bridgewater, Massachusetts, and sentenced to fifteen years' imprisonment.

The appeal to the Governor was presented by counsel for the accused on May 3rd of the present year. It was my first official connection with the case.

This appeal, presented to me in accordance with the provision in the Constitution of our Commonwealth, has been considered without intent on my part to sustain the courts if I became convinced that an error had been committed or that the trial had been unfair to the accused.

I realized at the outset that there were many sober-minded and conscientious men and women who were genuinely troubled about the guilt or innocence of the accused and the

231

fairness of their trial. It seemed to me I ought to attempt to set the minds of such people at rest, if it could be done, but I realized that with all I could do personally to find out the truth, some people might well in the end doubt the correctness of any conclusion that I, or in fact any other one man, might reach. I believed that I could best reassure these honest doubters by having a committee conduct an investigation entirely independent of my own, their report to be made to me and to be of help in reaching correct conclusions. I felt that if after such a committee had conducted its investigation independently we were not in substantial agreement, then the course of Massachusetts justice did not flow in as clear a channel as I believed it should. The final decision and responsibility was, of course, mine. For this committee I desired men who were not only well and favorably known for their achievements in their own lines, but men whose reputations for intelligence, open-mindedness, intellectual honesty and good judgment were above reproach. I asked to serve on that committee President Abbott Lawrence Lowell of Harvard University, former Judge Robert Grant, and President Samuel W. Stratton of Massachusetts Institute of Technology. No one of them hesitated when asked to serve. They began work as soon as their other affairs could be arranged, labored continuously during much of June and through July, holding their sessions independently, and arrived unanimously at a conclusion which is wholly in accord with mine. The public owes these gentlemen its gratitude for their highminded, unselfish service on this disagreeable and extremely important problem.

The court proceedings in this case may be divided into two parts: first, the trial before the jury with Judge Thayer presiding; second, the hearings on the succession of motions for a new trial which were addressed to the judge and passed upon by him. All those proceedings have been attacked by some of the friends of the accused men and their counsel.

The attacks on the jury trial take two forms:—first, it is asserted that the men are innocent and that there was not sufficient evidence before the jury to justify a finding of guilty; second, it is asserted that the trial was unfair. The attacks on the proceedings and on the motions for a new trial are in substance that the judge was biased and unable to give the motions fair and impartial consideration.

The inquiry that I have conducted has had to do with the following questions:—

Was the jury trial fair?

'Were the accused entitled to a new trial?

Are they guilty or not guilty?

As to the first question, complaint has been made that the defendants were prosecuted and convicted because they were anarchists. As a matter of fact, the issue of anarchy was brought in by them as an explanation of their suspicious conduct. Their counsel, against the advice of Judge Thayer, decided to attribute their actions and conduct to the fact that they were anarchists, suggesting that they were armed to protect themselves, that they were about to start out, at ten o'clock at night, to collect radical literature, and that the reason they lied was to save their friends.

I have consulted with every member of the jury now alive, eleven in number. They considered the judge fair; that he gave them no indication of his own opinion of the case. Affidavits have been presented claiming that the judge was prejudiced. I see no evidence of prejudice in his conduct of the trial. That he had an opinion as to the guilt or innocence of the accused after hearing the evidence is natural and inevitable.

The allegation has been made that conditions in the court room were prejudicial to the accused. After careful inquiry of the jury and others, I find no evidence to support this allegation. I find the jurors were thoroughly honest men and that they were reluctant to find these men guilty but were forced to do so by the evidence. I can see no warrant for the assertion that the jury trial was unfair.

The charge of the judge was satisfactory to the counsel for the accused and no exceptions were taken to it. The Supreme Judicial Court for the Commonwealth has considered such of the more than 250 exceptions taken during the course of the trial as counsel for the accused chose to argue and over-ruled them all, thus establishing that the proceedings were without legal flaw.

I have read the record and examined many witnesses and the jurymen to see from a layman's standpoint whether the trial was fairly conducted. I am convinced that it was.

The next question is whether newly discovered evidence was of sufficient merit to warrant a new trial.

After the verdict against these men, their counsel filed and argued before Judge Thayer seven distinct supplementary motions for a new trial six of them on the ground of newly discovered evidence, all of which were denied. I have examined all of these motions and read the affidavits in support of them to see whether they presented any valid reason for granting the accused men a new trial. I am convinced that they do not and I am further convinced that the presiding judge gave no evidence of bias in denying them all and refusing a new trial. The Supreme Judicial Court for the Commonwealth, which had before it appeals on four of the motions and had the opportunity to read the same affidavits which were submitted to Judge Thayer, declined to sustain the contentions of counsel for the accused. In my own investigations on the question of guilt, I have given these motions and their supporting affidavits and the witnesses every consideration.

I give no weight to the Madeiros confession. It is popularly supposed he confessed to committing this crime. In his testimony to me he could not recall the details or describe the neighborhood. He furthermore stated that the Government had doublecrossed him and he proposes to doublecross the Government. He feels that the District Attorney's office has treated him unfairly because his two confederates who were associated with him in the commission of the murder for which he was convicted were given life sentences, whereas he was sentenced to death. He confessed the crime for which he was convicted. I am not impressed with his knowledge of the South Braintree murders.

It has been a difficult task to look back six years through other people's eyes. Many of the witnesses told me their story in a way I felt was more a matter of repetition than the product of their memory. Some witnesses replied that during the six years they had forgotten; they could not remember; that it was a disagreeable experience and they had tried to forget it. I could not hope to put myself in the position of a juryman and have the advantage of seeing the witness on the stand and listening to the evidence and judging the spoken word. The motions for a new trial, however, were all made from affidavits and therefore they could be reviewed under the same circumstances as prevailed when the Judge heard them.

The next question, and the most vital question of all, is that of the guilt or innocence of the accused. In this connection I reviewed the Bridgewater attempted holdup for which Vanzetti had previously been tried before another jury and found guilty. At this trial Vanzetti did not take the witness stand in his own defense. He waived the privilege of telling his own story to the jury, and did not subject himself to cross examination. Investigating this case, I talked to the counsel for Vanzetti at the Plymouth trial, the jurymen, the trial witnesses, new witnesses, present counsel and Vanzetti. I have talked with the government witnesses who saw the Bridgewater holdup and who identified Vanzetti, and I believe their testimony to be substantially correct. I believe with the jury that Vanzetti was guilty and that his trial was fair. I found nothing unusual about this case except, as noted above, that Vanzetti did not testify.

In the Bridgewater case, practically everyone who witnessed the attempted holdup and who could have identified the bandits identified Vanzetti.

The South Braintree crime was particularly brutal. The murder of the paymaster (Parmenter) and the guard (Berardelli) was not necessary to the robbery. The murders were accomplished first, the robbery afterward. The first shot laid Berardelli low in the roadway, and after Parmenter was shot, he dropped the money box in the road and ran across the street. The money could then have been taken but the murderers pursued Parmenter across the road and shot him again, and then returned and fired three more shots into Berardelli, four in all, leaving his lifeless form in the roadway. The plan was evidently to kill the witnesses and terrorize the bystanders. The murderers escaped in an automobile driven by one of their confederates, the automobile being afterward located in the woods at Bridgewater, 18 miles distant.

Vanzetti when arrested on May 5th had in his hip pocket a fully loaded revolver. Sacco had a loaded pistol tucked into the front of his trousers and 20 loose cartridges which fitted this pistol. Upon being questioned by the police, both men told what they afterward admitted was a tissue of lies. Sacco claimed to have been working at Kelly's shoe factory on April 15th, the date of the South Braintree crime. Upon investigation, it was proven that he was not at work on that day. He then claimed to have been at the Italian Consulate in Boston on that date but the only confirmation of this claim is the memory of a former employee of the Consulate who made a deposition in Italy that Sacco among forty others was in the office that day. This employee had no memorandum to assist his memory.

As the result of my study of the record and my personal investigation of the case, including my interviews with a large number of witnesses, I believe, with the jury, that Sacco and Vanzetti were guilty and that the trial was fair.

This crime was committed seven years ago. For six years, through dilatory methods, one appeal after another, every possibility for delay has been utilized, all of which lends itself to attempts to frighten and coerce witnesses, to influence changes in testimony, to multiply by the very years of time elapsed the possibilities of error and confusion.

It might be said that by undertaking this investigation I

have contributed to the elaborate consideration accorded these men. My answer is that there was a feeling on the part of some people that the various delays that had dragged this case through the courts for six years were evidence that a doubt existed as to the guilt of these two men. The feeling was not justified. The persistent, determined efforts of an attorney of extraordinary versatility and industry, the judge's illness, the election efforts of three District Attorneys, and dilatoriness on the part of most of those concerned are the principal causes of delay. The delays that have dragged this case out for six years are inexcusable.

This task of review has been a laborious one and I am proud to be associated in this public service with clear-eyed witnesses, unafraid to tell the truth, and with jurors who discharged their obligations in accordance with their convictions and their oaths.

As a result of my investigation I find no sufficient justification for executive intervention.

I believe with the jury, that these men, Sacco and Vanzetti, were guilty, and that they had a fair trial. I furthermore believe that there was no justifiable reason for giving them a new trial.

ALVAN T. FULLER

THE FOLLOWING PHOTOSTAT
REPRODUCES A LETTER WRITTEN BY
JOE MORELLI TO MORRIS L. ERNST,
ESQUIRE ("DEAR MR. MORRIS").

Joseph Morelli                          Jan. 19, 1939,
70 Toledo Ave.
Pawtucket, R.I.

Dear Mr. Morris:

My Attorney James H. Kiernan advise me to write
to you regarding to the Sacco-Vanzetti case.

Now here is the dope. Jan. 13 1933, I wascentenced
to five years to U.S. Northeastern Penitentiary Lewisburg,
Pa. While there I wrote the history of my life, including
the Sacco- Vanzetti case, and many more cases. My Manuscript
contains of 574 pages. Now if you are interested to put
my story on the market i'm sure the book would sell like
hot cakes. Have you read Al Capone's book, his book would
not compare with my. You must remember that I been in the
racket 40 years and still, *even* therefore I must have something
to tell. If you were to read the history of my life your
hair would stand straight up under your hat. i'll be 62
year old nest month, and I don't look a day over 40.
Now if you are intersted in the Sacco-Vanzetti case, and
want the real truth and not baloney, than you can write
me at my home. If you wish to come to my home you can do so.
And if you want me to come to see you i'll come there.
I know that/*my* story will make plenty of money for you and me.

Yours Truly

*Joseph Morelli*

FROM THE PROCEEDINGS BEFORE

THE COUNCIL AND MEMBERS OF

THE BAR ASSOCIATION OF THE

CITY OF BOSTON, IN MEMORY OF

WILLIAM G. THOMPSON,

MARCH 19, 1938.

HERBERT B. EHRMANN, ESQUIRE:

I SHALL not here attempt to discuss William G. Thompson as an outstanding member of the Boston bar. No such tribute of mine would approach in truth and beauty the memorial prepared by Damon Hall. Nor shall I speak particularly of his personal traits or public service, since there are those here today better qualified to lay these wreaths upon his memory. It was, however, my fortune to share with Thompson the tragic experience of the Sacco-Vanzetti case. I knew at first hand his constant courtesy and generosity toward a younger associate and his sustaining courage in the face of cruel disappointment. Particularly, I observed the effect of those stirring years upon his character, and it is that development, in my opinion, which has made Thompson's life so full of meaning for his friends. In discussing this matter I have

239

no intention or desire to stir up emotions that have long since happily subsided. It would be inappropriate, however, in considering Thompson's career, to leave out the most transforming event of his life.

Had Thompson been radical minded, the impact of the Sacco-Vanzetti case would have required no great emotional readjustment. But he was, and remained to the end, a genuine conservative, believing that mankind is better served through progress in the existing order rather than by sudden change or drastic experimentation. He had faith in private property, in the material rewards for effort and capacity, in the church as an institution. He desired the good opinion of his fellow men and was sensitive to adverse criticism. He had the New England virtues of thrift, thoroughness, and independence. He valued democracy because theoretically it gave the tools to him who could handle them. But with these beliefs went the assumption that there were certain standards of conduct that differentiated a free society from a dog fight. Those who reached the top in such an order, whether through the acquisition of education, wealth, or power, had a corresponding obligation to use these advantages like gentlemen. This code did not permit the cultured to scorn the ignorant, the rich to increase their means by abusing their privileged position, the powerful to deny fair play to the weak. Such things occurred, of course, but they were not accepted in the world as he saw it. It was this faith in the reality of *noblesse oblige* that was to be undermined by the Sacco-Vanzetti case.

Few had suspected the smouldering fires in Thompson's soul. To all appearances, he was merely another successful trial lawyer distinguished chiefly for his keen intellect, his classical background, and a modest, but adequate, sense of public duty. He had not wished to represent Sacco and Vanzetti. When asked to be their lawyer after the trial was over, he named a retainer large enough, as he thought, to remove the case from his office. To his surprise these terms were accepted and Thompson was launched on the most desperate struggle of his career, which he was destined to carry on

long after funds, hope, and physical vitality were alike
exhausted.

At first Thompson was confident that he would save the
men. It was not merely that he believed in his case or in the
soundness of his exceptions. He felt that the hostile atmosphere of the trial and the personality of the judge were such
that the unfairness of the whole proceeding was obvious to
any informed person—an opinion later expressed by Mr.
Justice Holmes and many fellow members of the bar. This
being so, he was sure that the code he believed to exist would
never permit men so convicted to be sent to their death. His
first shock came when some of his acquaintances not only
failed to share his view but actually evinced a coolness toward him for defending the men. Then, as motion after motion was denied and he was unable to get a review of any of
the trial judge's decisions on these matters, he was finally
gripped by the realization that his efforts were all in vain.
I believe that this conviction came to him during the argument on the exceptions in January, 1927. We had gone directly to his office from the courthouse and he had been
cheering me, as his young associate, by pointing out the apparently encouraging attitude of some of the justices. I said
good-by and left his office but returned unexpectedly after a
few moments. He did not look up but, mistaking my tread
for that of his partner, George Mears, expressed his real
thought in a voice broken with emotion.

"There is no hope, Mr. Mears—no hope."

Thereafter Thompson gave up his grave effort at encour-
agement and openly expressed his fears. On several occasions
he observed that events were moving with the classic inevita-
bility of the Phaedo, little suspecting that he himself was
destined to give point to the comparison by chronicling his
now celebrated last interview with Vanzetti. Nevertheless, it
was this realization of hopelessness that finally kindled
Thompson's powerful nature. He had believed in those An-
glo-Saxon ideals of justice that in the past had found expression in the history and constitution of Massachusetts. It

mortified him that persons enjoying all the advantages our civilization could offer should accept the idea that it was better for Sacco and Vanzetti to die, even if innocent, than for the Commonwealth to admit a mistake under fire. He looked at the world in which he had put so much faith. It appeared prosperous, satisfied, and irresistible. Yet something had gone out of such a society, and Thompson knew what it was. The sense of being personally let down lent him an emotional drive that carried him on.

His scrutiny passed from those persons directly concerned in the Sacco-Vanzetti case to the entire public service. There he thought he detected widespread shoddiness and mediocrity. He sensed the decided drift toward the view that public office is the private property of those who win elections, to be distributed to friends and supporters quite regardless of qualifications. Long before the revelations that followed the debacle of 1929, he saw that many leaders of business and finance were dealing with ethical standards as mere rules of convenience. In his lighter moments, he deplored the lack of an aristocracy that could restrain what he called "the shopkeeper's mentality." There was no one, he would say, to check the question, "What is there in it for me," with the gentleman's query, "What is the decent thing to do?" Economic formulas for saving society did not appeal to him. People could be unfair, cruel, and unjust under any system. What was needed most was a fresh appreciation of that almost forgotten virtue—character.

A weaker man might have been content merely to grumble at conditions. Thompson, in the seventh decade of his life, set out to change them. Soon his indignant voice was heard in many places. It was raised in the Council of this association. His dissents in the Massachusetts' Judicial Council warned repeatedly that improvements in the machinery of government were idle unless the appointing power paid more heed to capacity and integrity and less to politics. When there was an important judicial vacancy, he often personally besieged the governor until a well qualified man was named. His presence was frequently noted at legislative hearings where he sought laws to prevent ignorant officials from nullifying the Bill of Rights. He went on the hustings at election time, campaigning for those who he thought would best carry out his ideals. These things he did in addition to carrying on a busy practice at a time when most men feel they have earned the right to let others worry about the world. During part of the time he was seriously ill, and there can be no doubt that this gallant effort shortened his life.

There were compensations, however. His new activities brought him many contacts, and men and women from all walks of life became his friends. Economic and social status had ceased to have any meaning for him, and he found congenial minds everywhere. The explosion in his soul had brought to the surface hidden qualities of leadership, and he attracted a growing number of persons willing to assist him in his fight to lift the standards of Massachusetts. Had not sickness and death intervened, he might actually have succeeded in the unique one-man campaign he had begun so valiantly. But the Sacco-Vanzetti experience had come to him too late in life. It is for us who knew him well not to forget the lesson which he learned and taught.

# NOTE TO REMARKS OF

# HERBERT B. EHRMANN, ESQUIRE

Just before the beginning of the proceedings in memory of Mr. Thompson, I noticed that Justice Edward P. Pierce had entered the room. Justice Pierce had recently resigned from the Massachusetts Supreme Judicial Court on which he had served during the entire period covered by the Sacco and Vanzetti appeals and exceptions. Since what I was about to say might be understood by Justice Pierce to be critical of the Massachusetts Supreme Judicial Court, I felt somewhat uneasy as I began to talk.

After the proceedings were concluded, I saw the Justice approaching me, apparently under stress of a powerful emotion. The tears were pouring down his cheeks. To my amazement he grasped my hands warmly and said in a rather broken voice, "Thank you! Thank you! Thank you!"

The court on which Justice Pierce had served was presided over by Chief Justice Arthur P. Rugg. Rarely, if ever, did this court issue any dissenting opinion. We never knew what differences, if any, were expressed by the members of this court, during the formulation of opinions adverse to Sacco and Vanzetti. So far as I know, the very real emotion of Justice Pierce at the memorial proceedings for William G. Thompson provides our only glimpse behind the facade of apparent unity of this court which declined to disturb the jury's verdict or the discretionary decisions of Judge Webster Thayer.

H. B. E.

# VANZETTI'S LAST STATEMENT*

## A RECORD BY W. G. THOMPSON

*THIS RECORD was written by Mr. Thompson from notes he set down after his talk with Vanzetti on Monday, August 22, 1927, a few hours before the execution. He went directly from the death house of the Charlestown State Prison to his office and there transferred the experience to paper, while it was vivid in his mind. This record appeared in* The Atlantic Monthly *for February, 1928, and subsequently was reprinted in* The New Republic.

Sacco and Vanzetti were in the Death House in the State Prison at Charlestown. They fully understood that they were to die immediately after midnight. Mr. Ehrmann and I, having on their behalf exhausted every legal remedy which seemed to us available, had retired from the active conduct of the case, holding ourselves in readiness, however, to help their new counsel in any way we could.

I was in New Hampshire, where a message reached me from Vanzetti that he wanted to see me once more before he died. I immediately started for Boston with my son, reached the prison in the late afternoon or early evening, and was at once taken by the Warden to Vanzetti. He was in one of the three cells in a narrow room opening immediately to the

* Reprinted by courtesy of *The Atlantic Monthly*.

chair. In the cell nearest the chair was Madeiros, in the middle one Sacco, and in the third I found Vanzetti. There was a small table in his cell, and when I entered the room he seemed to be writing. The iron bars on the front of the cell were so arranged as to leave at one place a wider space, through which what he needed could be handed to him. Vanzetti seemed to be expecting me; and when I entered he rose from his table, and with his characteristic smile reached through the space between the bars and grasped me warmly by the hand. It was intimated to me that I might sit in a chair in front of the cell, but not nearer the bars than a straight mark painted on the floor. This I did.

I had heard that the Governor had said that if Vanzetti would release his counsel in the Bridgewater case from their obligation not to disclose what he had said to them the public would be satisfied that he was guilty of that crime, and also of the South Braintree crime. I therefore began the interview by asking one of the two prison guards who sat at the other end of the room, about fifteen feet from where we were, to come to the front of the cell and listen to the questions I was about to ask Vanzetti and to his replies. I then asked Vanzetti if he had at any time said anything to Mr. Vahey or Mr. Graham which would warrant the inference that he was guilty of either crime. With great emphasis and obvious sincerity he answered "no." He then said, what he had often said to me before, that Messrs. Vahey and Graham were not his personal choice, but became his lawyers at the urgent request of friends, who raised the money to pay them. He then told me certain things about their relations to him and about their conduct of the Bridgewater case, and what he had in fact told them. This on the next day I recorded, but will not here repeat.

I asked Vanzetti whether he would authorize me to waive on his behalf his privilege so far as Vahey and Graham were concerned. He readily assented to this, but imposed the condition that they should make whatever statement they saw fit to make in the presence of myself or some other friend, giving his reasons for this condition, which I also recorded.

The guard then returned to his seat.

I told Vanzetti that although my belief in his innocence had all the time been strengthened, both by my study of the evidence and by my increasing knowledge of his personality, yet there was a chance, however remote, that I might be mistaken; and that I thought he ought for my sake, in this closing hour of his life when nothing could save him, to give me his most solemn reassurance, both with respect to himself and with respect to Sacco. Vanzetti then told me quietly and calmly, and with a sincerity which I could not doubt, that I need have no anxiety about this matter; that both he and Sacco were absolutely innocent of the South Braintree crime, and that he (Vanzetti) was equally innocent of the Bridgewater crime; that while, looking back, he now realized more clearly than he ever had the grounds of the suspicion against him and Sacco, he felt that no allowance had been made for his ignorance of American points of view and habits of thought, or for his fear as a radical and almost as an outlaw, and that in reality he was convicted on evidence which would not have convicted him had he not been an anarchist, so that he was in a very real sense dying for his cause. He said it was a cause for which he was prepared to die. He said it was the cause of the upward progress of humanity, and the elimination of force from the world. He spoke with calmness, knowledge, and deep feeling. He said he was grateful to me for what I had done for him. He asked to be remembered to my wife and son. He spoke with emotion of his sister and of his family. He asked me to do what I could to clear his name, using the words "clear my name."

I asked him if he thought it would do any good for me or any friend to see Boda. He said he thought it would. He said he did not know Boda very well, but believed him to

be an honest man, and thought possibly he might be able to
give some evidence which would help to prove their innocence.

I then told Vanzetti that I hoped he would issue a public
statement advising his friends against retaliating by violence
and reprisal. I told him that, as I read history, the truth had
little chance of prevailing when violence was followed by
counter-violence. I said that as he well knew, I could not
subscribe to his views or to his philosophy of life; but that,
on the other hand, I could not but respect any man who
consistently lived up to altruistic principles, and was willing
to give his life for them. I said that if I were mistaken, and
if his views were true, nothing could retard their acceptance
by the world more than the hate and fear that would be
stirred up by violent reprisal. Vanzetti replied that, as I
must well know, he desired no personal revenge for the cruel-
ties inflicted upon him; but he said that, as he read history,
every great cause for the benefit of humanity had had to
fight for its existence against entrenched power and wrong,
and that for this reason he could not give his friends such
sweeping advice as I had urged. He added that in such
struggles he was strongly opposed to any injury to women
and children. He asked me to remember the cruelty of seven
years of imprisonment, with alternating hopes and fears.
He reminded me of the remarks attributed to Judge Thayer
by certain witnesses, especially by Professor Richardson,
and asked me what state of mind I thought such remarks
indicated. He asked me how any candid man could believe
that a judge capable of referring to men accused before him
as "anarchistic bastards" could be impartial, and whether
I thought that such refinement of cruelty as had been prac-
tised upon him and upon Sacco ought to go unpunished.

I replied that he well knew my own opinion of these
matters, but that his arguments seemed to me not to meet
the point I had raised, which was whether he did not prefer
the prevalence of his opinions to the infliction of punishment

upon persons, however richly he might think they deserved it. This led to a pause in the conversation.

Without directly replying to my question, Vanzetti then began to speak of the origin, early struggles, and progress of other great movements for human betterment. He said that all great altruistic movements originated in the brain of some man of genius, but later became misunderstood and perverted, both by popular ignorance and by sinister self-interest. He said that all great movements which struck at conservative standards, received opinions, established institutions, and human selfishness were at first met with violence and persecution. He referred to Socrates, Galileo, Giordano Bruno, and others whose names I do not now remember, some Italian and some Russian. He then referred to Christianity, and said that it began in simplicity and sincerity, which were met with persecution and oppression, but that it later passed quietly into ecclesiasticism and tyranny. I said I did not think that the progress of Christianity had been altogether checked by convention and ecclesiasticism, but that on the contrary it still made an appeal to thousands of simple people, and that the essence of the appeal was the supreme confidence shown by Jesus in the truth of His own views by forgiving, even when on the Cross, His enemies, persecutors, and slanderers.

Now, for the first and only time in the conversation, Vanzetti showed a feeling of personal resentment against his enemies. He spoke with eloquence of his sufferings, and asked me whether I thought it possible that he could forgive those who had persecuted and tortured him through seven years of inexpressible misery. I told him he knew how deeply I sympathized with him, and that I had asked him to reflect upon the career of One infinitely superior to myself and to him, and upon a force infinitely greater than the force of hate and revenge. I said that in the long run the force to which the world would respond was the force of love and not of hate, and that I was suggesting to him to forgive his enemies, not for their sakes, but for his own peace of mind, and also because an example of such forgiveness would in the end be more powerful to win adherence to his cause or to a belief in his innocence than anything else that could be done.

There was another pause in the conversation. I arose and we stood gazing at each other for a minute or two in silence. Vanzetti finally said that he would think of what I had said.[1]

I then made a reference to the possibility of personal immortality, and said that, although I thought I understood the difficulties of a belief in immortality, yet I felt sure that if there was a personal immortality he might hope to share it. This remark he received in silence.

He then returned to his discussion of the evil of the present organization of society, saying that the essence of the wrong was the opportunity it afforded persons who were powerful because of ability or strategic economic position to oppress the simple-minded and idealistic among their fellow men, and that he feared that nothing but violent resistance could ever overcome the selfishness which was the basis of the present organization of society and made the few willing to perpetuate a system which enabled them to exploit the many.

I have given only the substance of this conversation, but I think I have covered every point that was talked about and have presented a true picture of the general tenor of Vanzetti's remarks. Throughout the conversation, with the few exceptions I have mentioned, the thought that was uppermost in his mind was the truth of the ideas in which he believed for the betterment of humanity, and the chance they had of prevailing. I was impressed by the strength of Vanzetti's mind, and by the extent of his reading and knowledge. He

[1] It is credibly reported that when, a few hours later, Vanzetti was about to step in the chair, he paused, shook hands with the Warden and Deputy Warden and the guards, thanked them for their kindness to him, and, turning to the spectators, asked them to remember that he forgave some of his enemies.

did not talk like a fanatic. Although intensely convinced of the truth of his own views, he was still able to listen with calmness and with understanding to the expression of views with which he did not agree. In this closing scene the impression of him which had been gaining ground in my mind for three years was deepened and confirmed—that he was a man of powerful mind, and unselfish disposition, of seasoned character, and of devotion to high ideals. There was no sign of breaking down or of terror at approaching death. At parting he gave me a firm clasp of the hand and a steady glance, which revealed unmistakably the depth of his feeling and the firmness of his self-control.

I then turned to Sacco, who lay upon a cot bed in the adjoining cell and could easily have heard and undoubtedly did hear my conversation with Vanzetti. My conversation with Sacco was very brief. He rose from his cot, referred feelingly though in a general way to some points of disagreement between us in the past, said he hoped that our differences of opinion had not affected our personal relations, thanked me for what I had done for him, showed no sign of fear, shook hands with me firmly, and· bade me good-bye. His manner also was one of absolute sincerity. It was magnanimous in him not to refer more specifically to our previous differences of opinion, because at the root of it all lay his conviction, often expressed to me, that all efforts on his behalf, either in court or with public authorities, would be useless, because no capitalistic society could afford to accord him justice. I had taken the contrary view; but at this last meeting he did not suggest that the result seemed to justify his view and not mine.[2]

[2] I afterward talked with the prison guard to whom I have referred in this paper. He told me that after he returned to his seat he heard all that was said by Vanzetti and myself. The room was quiet and no other persons were talking. I showed the guard my complete notes of the interview, including what Vanzetti had told me about Messrs. Vahey and Graham. He read the notes carefully and said that they corresponded entirely with his memory except that I had omitted a remark made by Vanzetti about women and children. I then remembered the remark and added it to my memorandum.

# SELECTED LETTERS AND

## STATEMENTS OF

## SACCO AND VANZETTI*

*"If it had not been for these thing, I might have live out my life talking at street corners to scorning men. I might have die, unmarked, unknown, a failure. Now we are not a failure. This is our career and our triumph. Never in our full life could we hope to do such work for tolerance, for joostice, for man's onderstanding of man as now we do by accident. Our words—our lives— our pains—nothing! The taking of our lives—lives of a good shoemaker and a poor fish-peddler—all! That last moment belongs to us—that agony is our triumph."*

FROM A STATEMENT MADE BY VANZETTI
AFTER RECEIVING SENTENCE, APRIL 9, 1927.

*July 19, 1927. Charlestown State Prison*

MY DEAR INES:

I would like that you should understand what I am going to say to you, and I wish I could write you so plain, for I long so much to have you hear all the heart-beat eagerness of your father, for I love you so much as you are the dearest little beloved one.

It is quite hard indeed to make you understand in your

* From *The Letters of Sacco and Vanzetti.* Reprinted by permission of The Viking Press.

253

young age, but I am going to try from the bottom of my heart to make you understand how dear you are to your father's soul. If I cannot succeed in doing that, I know that you will save this letter and read it over in future years to come and you will see and feel the same heart-beat affection as your father feels in writing it to you.

I will bring with me your little and so dearest letter and carry it right under my heart to the last day of my life. When I die, it will be buried with your father who loves you so much, as I do also your brother Dante and holy dear mother.

You don't know Ines, how dear and great your letter was to your father. It is the most golden present that you could have given to me or that I could have wished for in these sad days.

It was the greatest treasure and sweetness in my struggling life that I could have lived with you and your brother Dante and your mother in a neat little farm, and learn all your sincere words and tender affection. Then in the summertime to be sitting with you in the home nest under the oak tree shade—beginning to teach you of life and how to read and write, to see you running, laughing, crying and singing through the verdant fields picking the wild flowers here and there from one tree to another, and from the clear, vivid stream to your mother's embrace.

The same I have wished to see for other poor girls, and their brothers, happy with their mother and father as I dreamed for us—but it was not so and the nightmare of the lower classes saddened very badly your father's soul.

For the things of beauty and of good in this life, mother nature gave to us all, for the conquest and the joy of liberty. The men of this dying old society, they brutally have pulled me away from the embrace of your brother and your poor mother. But, in spite of all, the free spirit of your father's faith still survives, and I have lived for it and for the dream that some day I would have come back to life, to the embrace of your dear mother, among our friends and comrades again, but woe is me!

I know that you are good and surely you love your mother, Dante and all the beloved ones—and I am sure that you love me also a little, for I love you much and then so much. You do not know Ines, how often I think of you every day. You are in my heart, in my vision, in every angle of this sad walled cell, in the sky and everywhere my gaze rests.

Meantime, give my best paternal greetings to all the friends and comrades, and doubly so to our beloved ones. Love and kisses to your brother and mother.

With the most affectionate kiss and ineffable caress from him who loves you so much that he constantly thinks of you. Best warm greetings from Bartolo to you all.

[*From Sacco to his daughter*]                    YOUR FATHER

*August 18, 1927. Charlestown State Prison*

MY DEAR SON AND COMPANION:

Since the day I saw you last I had always the idea to write you this letter, but the length of my hunger strike and the thought I might not be able to explain myself, made me put it off all this time.

The other day, I ended my hunger strike and just as soon as I did that I thought of you to write to you, but I find that I did not have enough strength and I cannot finish it at one time. However, I want to get it down in any way before they take us again to the death-house, because it is my conviction that just as soon as the court refuses a new trial to us they will take us there. And between Friday and Monday, if nothing happens, they will electrocute us right after midnight, on August 22nd. Therefore, here I am, right with you with love and with open heart as ever I was yesterday.

I never thought that our inseparable life could be separated, but the thought of seven dolorous years makes it seem it did come, but then it has not changed really the unrest and the heart-beat of affection. That has remained as it was. More. I say that our ineffable affection reciprocal, is today more than any other time, of course. That is not only a great deal but it is grand because you can see the real brotherly love, not only in joy but also and more in the struggle of suffering. Remember this, Dante. We have demonstrated this, and modesty apart, we are proud of it.

Much we have suffered during this long Calvary. We protest today as we protested yesterday. We protest always for our freedom.

If I stopped hunger strike the other day, it was because there was no more sign of life in me. Because I protested with my hunger strike yesterday as today I protest for life and not for death.

I sacrificed because I wanted to come back to the embrace of your dear little sister Ines and your mother and all the beloved friends and comrades of life and not death. So Son, today life begins to revive slow and calm, but yet without horizon and always with sadness and visions of death.

Well, my dear boy, after your mother had talked to me so much and I had dreamed of you day and night, how joyful it was to see you at last. To have talked with you like we used to in the days—in those days. Much I told you on that visit and more I wanted to say, but I saw that you will remain the same affectionate boy, faithful to your mother who loves you so much, and I did not want to hurt your sensibilities any longer, because I am sure that you will continue to be the same boy and remember what I have told you. I knew that and what here I am going to tell you will touch your sensibilities, but don't cry Dante, because many tears have been wasted, as your mother's have been wasted for seven years, and never did any good. So, Son, instead of crying, be strong, so as to be able to comfort your mother, and when you want to distract your mother from the discouraging soulness, I will tell you what I used to do. To take her for a long walk in the quiet country, gathering wild flowers here and there, resting under the shade of trees, between the harmony of the vivid stream and the gentle tranquility of the mothernature, and I am sure that she will enjoy this very much, as you surely would be happy for it. But remember always, Dante, in the play of happiness, don't you use all for yourself only, but down yourself just one step, at your side and help the weak ones that cry for help, help the prosecuted and the victim, because that are your better friends; they are the comrades that fight and fall as your father and Bartolo fought and fell yesterday for the conquest of the joy of freedom for all and the poor workers. In this struggle of life you will find more love and you will be loved.

I am sure that from what your mother told me about what you said during these last terrible days when I was lying in the iniquitous death-house—that description gave me happiness because it showed you will be the beloved boy I had always dreamed.

Therefore whatever should happen tomorrow, nobody knows, but if they should kill us, you must not forget to look at your friends and comrades with the smiling gaze of gratitude as you look at your beloved ones, because they love you as they love every one of the fallen persecuted comrades. I tell you, your father that is all the life to you, your father that loved you and saw them, and knows their noble faith (that is mine) their supreme sacrifice that they are still doing for our freedom, for I have fought with them, and they are the ones that still hold the last of our hope that today they can still save us from electrocution, it is the struggle and fight between the rich and the poor for safety and freedom, Son, which you will understand in the future of your years to come, of this unrest and struggle of life's death.

Much I thought of you when I was lying in the death house—the singing, the kind tender voices of the children from the playground, where there was all the life and the joy of liberty—just one step from the wall which contains the buried agony of three buried souls. It would remind me so often of you and your sister Ines, and I wish I could see you every moment. But I feel better that you did not come to the death-house so that you could not see the horrible picture of three lying in agony waiting to be electrocuted, because I do not know what effect it would have on your young age. But then, in another way if you were not so sensitive it would be very useful to you tomorrow when you could use this horrible memory to hold up to the world the shame of the country in this cruel persecution and unjust death. Yes, Dante, they can crucify our bodies today as they are doing, but they cannot destroy our ideas, that will remain for the youth of the future to come.

Dante, when I said three human lives buried, I meant to say that with us there is another young man by the name of Celestino Maderios that is to be electrocuted at the same time with us. He has been twice before in that horrible death-house, that should be destroyed with the hammers of real progress—that horrible house that will shame forever the future of the citizens of Massachusetts. They should destroy that house and put up a factory or school, to teach many of the hundreds of the poor orphan boys of the world.

Dante, I say once more to love and be nearest to your mother and the beloved ones in these sad days, and I am sure that with your brave heart and kind goodness they will feel less discomfort. And you will also not forget to love me a little for I do—O, Sonny! thinking so much and so often of you.

Best fraternal greetings to all the beloved ones, love and kisses to your little Ines and mother. Most hearty affectionate embrace,

YOUR FATHER AND COMPANION

P.S. Bartolo send you the most affectionate greetings. I hope that your mother will help you to understand this letter because I could have written much better and more simple, if I was feeling good. But I am so weak.

[*From Sacco to his son*]

*August 21, 1927. From the Death House*
*of Massachusetts State Prison*

MY DEAR DANTE:

I still hope, and we will fight until the last moment, to revindicate our right to live and to be free, but all the forces of the State and of the money and reaction are deadly against us because we are libertarians or anarchists.

I write little of this because you are now and yet too young to understand these things and other things of which I would like to reason with you.

But, if you do well, you will grow and understand your father's and my case and your father's and my principles, for which we will soon be put to death.

I tell you now that all that I know of your father, he is not a criminal, but one of the bravest men I ever knew. Some day you will understand what I am about to tell you. That your father has sacrificed everything dear and sacred to the human heart and soul for his fate in liberty and justice for all. That day you will be proud of your father, and if you come brave enough, you will take his place in the struggle between tyranny and liberty and you will vindicate his (our) names and our blood.

If we have to die now, you shall know, when you will be able to understand this tragedy in its fullest, how good and brave your father has been with you, your father and I, during these eight years of struggle, sorrow, passion, anguish and agony.

Even from now you shall be good, brave with your mother, with Ines, and with Susie—brave, good Susie [1] — and do all you can to console and help them.

I would like you to also remember me as a comrade and friend to your father, your mother and Ines, Susie and you, and I assure you that neither have I been a criminal, that

[1] Faithful friend of Mrs. Sacco, with whom she and her children lived during the last years of the case.

I have committed no robbery and no murder, but only fought modestly to abolish crimes from among mankind and for the liberty of all.

Remember Dante, each one who will say otherwise of your father and I, is a liar, insulting innocent dead men who have been brave in their life. Remember and know also, Dante, that if your father and I would have been cowards and hypocrits and rinnegetors of our faith, we would not have been put to death. They would not even have convicted a lebbrous dog; not even executed a deadly poisoned scorpion on such evidence as that they framed against us. They would have given a new trial to a matricide and abitual felon on the evidence we presented for a new trial.

Remember, Dante, remember always these things; we are not criminals; they convicted us on a frame-up; they denied us a new trial; and if we will be executed after seven years, four months and seventeen days of unspeakable tortures and wrong, it is for what I have already told you; because we were for the poor and against the exploitation and oppression of the man by the man.

The documents of our case, which you and other ones will collect and preserve, will prove to you that your father, your mother, Ines, my family and I have sacrificed by and to a State Reason of the American Plutocratic reaction.

The day will come when you will understand the atrocious cause of the above written words, in all its fullness. Then you will honor us.

Now Dante, be brave and good always. I embrace you.

P. S. I left the copy of *An American Bible* to your mother now, for she will like to read it, and she will give it to you when you will be bigger and able to understand it. Keep it for remembrance. It will also testify to you how good and generous Mrs. Gertrude Winslow has been with us all. Goodbye Dante.

BARTOLOMEO

# AFTER FORTY YEARS

A NOTE ON MR. ROBERT H. MONTGOMERY'S BOOK ENTITLED
*Sacco-Vanzetti, The Murder and The Myth.*

ROBERT H. MONTGOMERY's book devotes a great deal
of space to try to persuade its readers that *The Untried
Case* is an unconvincing narrative.

As this new edition is just going to press, there is no
time now for a comprehensive analysis of Mr. Montgomery's work, which seems to suffer from all of the
defects of violent and emotional partisanship. Nor do
I wish to dwell upon the derogatory tone of Mr. Montgomery's remarks concerning me, since, in this regard,
I share his sarcasm with my senior, the late William G.
Thompson, Mr. Justice Frankfurter, and others with
whom I am proud to be so associated.

The following few observations concerning Mr.
Montgomery's treatment of the material contained in
*The Untried Case* may indicate the character of his
book. Mr. Montgomery ignores the impact of the whole
of the evidence tending to corroborate the confession
of Madeiros, a series of revelations utterly impossible
to explain on the ground of coincidence. Instead, he

261

attacks each item separately. I shall follow his in-appropriate procedure.

When, in 1926, we first started to investigate the con-fession of Celestino Madeiros, that he, with a group of professional criminals, committed the crimes for which Sacco and Vanzetti were convicted, we had been unable to obtain any identification of his alleged associates. Madeiros had said that Italians were involved, that the gang centered in Providence, that they had been rob-bing freight cars of shoes and textiles and sending them to New York. However, it took only a quick visit to Providence to learn Madeiros had implicated the no-torious Morelli gang of that city. Their trial in the federal court for the freight-car robberies had been a local sensation.

A visit to New Bedford then disclosed some startling information. What we found in that city is related in Chapter IV of *The Untried Case*, "Sergeant Jacobs' Notebook." Mr. Montgomery gives some account of this (pp. 248–249, 265), but omits the all-important fact that in 1920, at the time of the South Braintree crimes, the police of New Bedford had suspected the Morellis of these crimes. When my friend John F. Stokes, in the 1940s, then Commissioner of Public Safety for Massachusetts, read *The Untried Case*, he made the following comment to me: "I am a police-man, and the one thing that has shaken me more than anything else is the fact that Madeiros, in 1926, pointed the finger at a gang actually suspected by the New Bed-

ford police when the search was on in 1920 for the
South Braintree murderers." Mr. Montgomery, however, terms the New Bedford story "unsatisfactory"
(p. 266). He prefers his own inexpert opinion to
such an extent that he rejects and ignores the contem-
porary attitude of the New Bedford police.

If the reader will turn to my Chapter III, "Pay Dirt
in Providence," he will see that five counts in the indictment against the Morellis were for having in their
possession shoes stolen from the very South Braintree factories in front of which the paymaster and the
guard were murdered. Since we also learned that the
gang posted a member at the point of shipment to note
the freight cars later to be "cracked" in the Providence
yards, such a "spotter" would have observed the entire
payroll procedure, the removal of the payroll from the
train to the express office, and its delivery to the shoe
factories. Here was a direct link to the very scene of
the crime, inscribed in court records six years before
Madeiros implicated the gang in the South Braintree
killings.

How does Mr. Montgomery present this ineradicable
fact? First he gives it the "shaggy dog" treatment—
there weren't so very many stolen shoes, only 683
pairs, and, besides, they were merely in the possession
of the Morellis (p. 244, p. 271). (The Morellis' operation was, in fact, big business. Although absolutely
irrelevant, any good prosecutor could have explained
to Mr. Montgomery why the indictment was limited to

specific lots of shoes still in the possession of the thieves.) Mr. Montgomery then exorcises the "spotter" as a "figment" of my imagination (p. 271). The solid basis establishing the presence of a "spotter" is set out on pages 49 to 54 in this book. Ignoring the actual facts, Mr. Montgomery simply asserts the Morellis did not need a "spotter," since they were stealing from freight cars in Providence. According to his own idea of the techniques of these robbers, they would have to open every freight car in the yards looking for shoes and textiles. To Mr. Montgomery it was ridiculous to suggest that they spotted shipments of shoes—it would be different, he argues, if they were robbing freight cars of diamonds (p. 271)! The reader may decide what kind of factless figment this fancy presents.

Again, if the reader will turn to the chapter in this book, "Prison Voices," he will learn that Joseph Morelli's close friend, Tony Mancini, killed a man in 1920 with a peculiar foreign weapon, of 7.65 millimeter calibre firing a .32 calibre bullet. It was listed on the District Attorney's records as a "Star." This was precisely the type of weapon that two experts had testified was used by the unknown killer in South Braintree. It was not contended that either defendant had fired this pistol. The background of the expert testimony is set out in detail on pages 119 to 124 of this book. One of the experts had thought the foreign automatic was a "Steyr." On page 123 of this book, I reported that the word "Star" in the Mancini record might possibly have been a mistake for "Steyr," but that it did not matter much, since the type, not the name, was crucial.

Mr. Montgomery disposes of the Mancini pistol in a few sentences (p. 264, p. 276) and then erroneously asserts that its significance depended on my "imagining that there was a stenographic error in the records of the District Attorney's Office." This misstatement completely obscures the startling corroboration of Madeiros, namely, the discovery that one of the Morelli gang, a ruthless killer, had in 1920 used to commit murder a peculiar weapon that experts in the Sacco-Vanzetti case testified had been used in South Braintree.

On page 270 Mr. Montgomery states:

"There was evidence that Sacco and Vanzetti were in possession of the stolen money immediately after the murders and during the getaway."

This is an inexcusably misleading statement. It occurs in a discussion by Mr. Montgomery concerning the possession of stolen money as proof of guilt. Taken in its context, this statement says there was evidence that identified Sacco and Vanzetti as the robbers, because at the time of the robbery and getaway they were found to have possession of the stolen money. There never was a shred of such evidence.*

* Sacco and Vanzetti were arrested on an interurban streetcar after an unsuccessful attempt to retrieve an old Overland car from the Johnson garage, although, according to Mr. Montgomery, they were already in possession of more than $15,000 and at least two automobiles.

Blindness to the facts permeates the entire book. For instance, unable to deny the testimony that Judge Thayer boasted of what he had done to those "anarchistic bastards" while he was still considering issues involving their life or death, Mr. Montgomery decides that Judge Thayer did not mean Sacco and Vanzetti, but their lawyer, Moore, and two other fellows, neither of whom was a victim of Judge Thayer's decisions and neither of whom was an anarchist (p. 315).

A piece of evidence the District Attorney and Judge Thayer thought very important was a cap produced at the trial and claimed to have belonged to Sacco. Emphasis was placed heavily on the fact that Sacco hung his own cap on a nail and that the cap in evidence had a tear in the lining. However, in 1927, Jeremiah F. Gallivan, Chief of Police of South Braintree, testified that he himself had torn the lining of the cap looking for identification marks. Unable to face the fact that the Commonwealth had put the cap in evidence without calling Mr. Gallivan to explain the tear, Mr. Montgomery then "finds" that the cap in evidence was not the one delivered to Chief Gallivan (p. 112). (Chief Gallivan testified that he saw it at the trial.) According to Mr. Montgomery, therefore, there must have been two caps, each found at the scene of the crime, each given into the possession of Mr. Fraher (superintendent of the Slater and Morrill factory), and each having a tear in the lining.

Again, confronted with the testimony of Elias Field

that Captain Proctor had stated in his presence that in Proctor's opinion the mortal bullet had not passed through Sacco's pistol, Mr. Montgomery, who apparently respects Mr. Field's integrity, baldly states that Field's recollection was defective (p. 230). Furthermore, Mr. Montgomery withholds from his readers the rest of Mr. Field's report concerning what Captain Proctor (the head of the Massachusetts State Police and a government expert at the trial) had added (Holt,* p. 4975):

"I have been too old in the game, I have been too long in the game, and I'm getting to be too old to want to see a couple of fellows go to the chair for something I don't think they did." *

The reader may judge whether these words represent more defective recollection by Mr. Field or something painful that Mr. Montgomery does not care to remember.

Mr. Montgomery's book relies often and heavily on the analysis of the evidence by Professor Edmund M. Morgan, who has been kind enough to write an introduction to this edition of *The Untried Case*. However, Mr. Montgomery fails to give his readers Professor Morgan's conclusion:

* *The Sacco-Vanzetti Case, Transcript of the Record of the Trial of Nicola Sacco and Bartolomeo Vanzetti in the Courts of Massachusetts and Subsequent Proceedings, 1920–7*, New York, Henry Holt & Company, 1928.

". . . that these defendants (Sacco and Vanzetti) were the victims of a tragic miscarriage of justice." *

There is much, much more of this sort of thing. However, the outstanding feature of Mr. Montgomery's book is not the mass of errors of commission and omission. It is his total lack of indignation about the many lapses from accepted standards for the administration of justice. Some of these he chronicles, but only to seek complacent explanations and justifications. His anger is reserved only for sympathizers with Sacco and Vanzetti. He assails the most unimpeachable evidence that favors the men but cites with approval the reliance of the Lowell Commission upon the crazy story of a deranged woman (p. 220), whom even the prosecution rejected as a witness. He can accuse William G. Thompson, a leader of the Boston bar and the soul of honor—long after his death—of fabricating evidence (p. 316) but can utter no word of criticism as he records the fact that Judge Thayer invented nonexistent question-and-answer testimony to justify one of his decisions dooming Sacco and Vanzetti (p. 340).

* *The Legacy of Sacco and Vanzetti*, by Jonghin and Morgan, Harcourt, Brace and Company, 1948, p. 157.

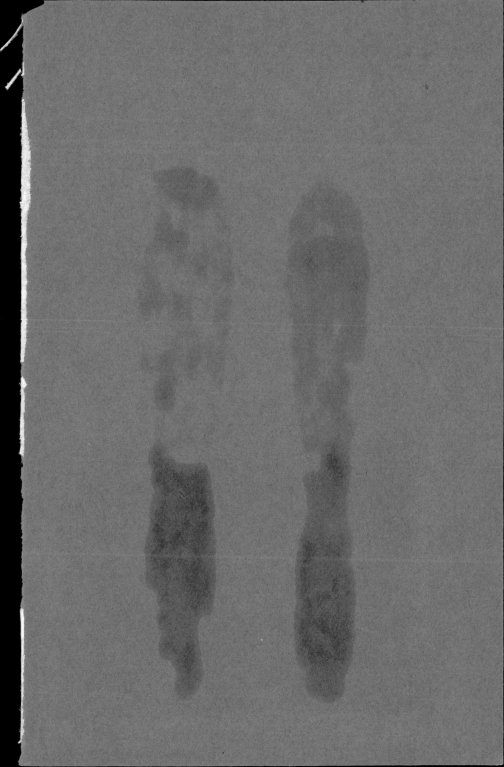